# THE TRAMWAYS OF THE
# WEST OF ENGLAND

# The

# Tramways of the

# West of England

## by

## P. W. Gentry

Published in London by
THE LIGHT RAILWAY TRANSPORT LEAGUE,
245-7, Cricklewood Broadway,
N.W.2.

First   Edition,   1952.

Second   Edition,   1960.

Printed in Great Britain
by
W. J. FOWLER & SON, LTD.,
Cricklewood Broadway,
London, N.W.2.
7001.

# PREFACE

FOR those many lovers of tramways—and they are greater in numbers than most imagine—it is a sad fact that these islands of ours constitute the only country of any importance in which the electric tramcar has ceased to be the chief form of urban street transport and is in danger of near-extinction within the foreseeable future. The all-conquering and ubiquitous bus has caught the public fancy and the trams in all too many places have been driven to the scrap yard. The causes of their decline in the past 20 years or so have already been analysed elsewhere and need not, therefore, be detailed here except in so far as the West of England is concerned, for nowhere has this changeover become so utterly a *fait accompli* than in the West Country where today there remains not a single tram in operation, not a stretch of line that is not tarred over and pounded upon by the wheels of their conquerors.

The reason for this is primarily the preponderance of narrow streets and consequently of single track in most West Country towns and cities, and the absence of the mass-transport requirements such as are present in the heavy industrial areas and which trams have been found best suited to handle. Thus, only Bristol and Plymouth presented traffic needs large enough to warrant the retention of tramways as a policy, and both had to contend with legal and technical difficulties which made that course seem impracticable and the quick and easy alternative of buses all the more attractive. It must be admitted that places like Cheltenham, Taunton and Swindon were not at all suited for trams in the face of present-day traffic conditions, and, indeed, if the motor bus had been developed 20 years earlier, they probably would never have had them at all. Something, however, could and should have been done with the popular sea-front lines at Weston and Torquay, since a " ride on the tram " always seems more fun at holiday times (particularly to the youngsters) than one on the work-a-day and un-inspiring bus, and Blackpool-type cars could have worked wonders had they been given a chance. Even the best bits of the Bath system were not without possibilities under skilful planning.

They were a most interesting assortment, these 12 West Country systems, and yet, strange to say, the one thing they had in common was that not one of them had a single top-covered car! Indeed, Plymouth and Exeter were still building open-toppers only a few years before London's modern "Felthams" first appeared on the scene to startle the transport world. This again may be ascribed to narrow streets and the consequent enforced use of the 3 ft. 6 in. gauge in many cases—yet have not Birmingham, Coventry and other places operated large fleets of top-covered cars on that gauge with perfect safety? Moreover, the standard gauge group (Bristol, Bath and Weston) likewise failed to give their customers a roof over their heads! Nevertheless, the fleets herein described included a good variety of rolling stock and the importation by Bristol, Cheltenham and Devonport of cars from America is worth noting.

The pioneer spirit of the West was well in evidence on its tramways as in so many other fields of enterprise. Bristol pointed the way to electrification in other cities; tiny Camborne and Redruth was one of the first and only lines of its type in Britain to cater specially for mineral traffic, while Cheltenham passengers sat on upholstery when most other folks had to be content with wooden seats!

But all that is now past and as the years advance, memories of tramway days in the West grow dim. It was, therefore, the writer's desire to set down a detailed account of them before spring turn-outs dispose of too many old records and while we still have with us those old-timers who proudly drove horse-cars along ill-paved streets and can tell us about riding in the first electric tram with all its wonders of a new age.

It is difficult—nay, almost impossible—to produce such an account without unwittingly making some errors, particularly as recollections (and even records!) have a habit of being at variance, and the writer would welcome advice of any that my be detected herein. With a view to easier reference, the articles have been arranged alphabetically and the data assembled under headings, which it is hoped will prove helpful. Also, the maps have been standardised as far as possible, thanks to Mr. J. C. Gillham who has carefully redrawn my maps to a uniform scale and design in a style acceptable to the block maker. My thanks are also due to Mr. J. W. Fowler for much technical advice in the selection of photographs for block making, and without his help and encouragement, I doubt if this book would have got beyond the MS. stage.

To the many persons, including former tramwaymen and officials of transport undertakings, who have so kindly contributed information to this book, the writer extends his warmest thanks. He would in particular gratefully acknowledge the help given by the following: Major C. S. N. Walker of Gloucester, who spent many hours of his spare time in collaborating in the preparation of the book and was responsible for some of the maps; Mr. R. C. Sambourne of Plymouth, for valuable assistance on the Devonshire systems and other help; Mr.

S. Brenton and Mr. B. Y. Williams, who also contributed data on those systems; Mr. H. V. Jinks of Oxford for submitting material on Swindon and Worcester; Mr. R. S. Rumbold, M.Inst.T., Traffic Manager, Bristol Tramways & Carriage Co., Ltd.; Mr. H. C. Ludgate, General Manager, Swindon Corporation Passenger Transport Department; Mr. W. Y. Smith-Saville, M.Inst.T., formerly Engineer & General Manager, Exeter Corporation Transport Department; Mr. F. H. Corson, formerly General Manager & Engineer, Gloucester Corporation Light Railways; Mr. C. H. Built, formerly Manager and Engineer, Worcester Electric Traction Co., Ltd.; Mr. J. R. Burrell, Librarian, Camborne-Redruth Urban District Council; Mr. R. S. Hobbs, for the use of his collected data on the Bath tramways; and to Mr. N. P. Willis of Cheltenham and Mr. B. R. Miller of Portsmouth who very kindly undertook the task of editing the rolling stock data relating to the Cheltenham system. Certain data assembled by the late G. N. Southerden of Exeter has also been included, and reference has been made to the pages of ' The Modern Tramway,' ' Modern Transport,' and ' Railway Magazine,' and old editions of the local papers.

Thanks must also be tendered to all those who have lent or given photographs, and also to Mr. W. H. Bett, for much information on tickets and for the loan of so many, of which a selection is used, to illustrate this work.

A number of photographs by the late G. N. Southerden have been used, and for this the author desires to extend thanks to Mr. V. E. Burrows of Upminster who has acquired the collection and now administers the copyright.

P. W. GENTRY.

*　　*　　*

## PREFACE TO THE SECOND EDITION.

In writing this preface to the second edition, I would like to thank all those who wrote to me or my colleague Major Walker pointing out some errors, and to the many who wrote so appreciatively on my humble effort which I had hoped would pave the way for similar books on other parts of the country. The fact that the first edition sold out and still orders come in shows that interest still exists in a form of transport now unknown in the West of England for practically 25 years. In this edition some errors have been corrected, and some fresh photographs added, and while I personally have had little to do with this owing to private circumstances, I would like to thank all those who have made this second edition possible.

P. W. GENTRY.

Hazel Grove, Cheshire.
30th March, 1960.

# CONTENTS

STANDARD KEY
USED IN ALL MAPS

HORSE TRAMWAYS NOT ELECTRIFIED
ELECTRIC LINES, WITH TRACK LAYOUT
PROPOSED EXTENSIONS NOT BUILT
INTERLACED OR GAUNTLET TRACKS
CENTRE POLES BETWEEN TWO TRACKS
OTHER IMPORTANT ROADS
MAIN AND BRANCH RAILWAYS

# FOREWORD

## Major F. J. Chapple, D.S.O., O.B.E.

(Chairman, Bristol Tramways & Carriage Co., Ltd.)

I AM pleased to be asked to contribute this Foreword as, although I cannot claim to have been connected with the beginning and the end of Tramways, the statement would be true as regards the majority of those electrically operated, as it is now well over 50 years ago that I was first engaged on the electrification of tramways in Stoke-on-Trent. I have, in later years, been largely engaged in replacing them!

The tramways industry was large and important, and there are still many people who feel that the best case was not made for its continuance in many instances. The fact remains, however, that except for a very select few, operating mostly on reserved tracks, the tramway has practically vanished from the land.

As it may be claimed that tramway history is the history of local transport for nearly 100 years, it is, therefore, very fitting that this book should be published whilst there is still a generation that remembers tramways, and which includes many who have made tramways their hobby.

I have read the book with interest, and must congratulate all concerned on the general accuracy of the information it contains. It, quite rightly, is likely to remain the permanent and only complete historical note on the industry in the West of England.

June, 1952.

# BATH

## HORSE TRAMWAYS.

The Bath Road Car & Tramway Co., Ltd. operated a single line of horse tramway in this city, the route of which extended from the Great Western Railway Station to the Grosvenor College in London Road, via Southgate Street, Cheap Street, High Street and Walcot Street. The first car ran on Christmas Eve, 1880, but there is some doubt as to whether the whole of the line was opened at that time. An aged resident who remembers riding in the second or third car from Grosvenor College states that he could travel as far as Old Bridge, for which he paid a fare of twopence, and other statements have corroborated this. It would seem, therefore, that the Old Bridge to G.W.R. Station section was a later extension, and Keene's Bath Journal of 26th July, 1902, gives the route as G.W.R. to Grosvenor. This is in accord with the route length of 1 mile 57 chains as recorded by the Board of Trade.

The tramway was of 4 ft. gauge and was operated by seven cars, at least some of which were single-deckers; they were normally drawn by one horse each, but an extra horse was always attached in both directions between the top of Walcot Street and Cleveland Place where the route was rather steep. The depot and stables were built at the rear of the Porter Butt Hotel in Kensington, the building now being a British Restaurant. On Sundays the line was worked from Grosvenor as far as Old Bridge only. The service as advertised in 1900 ran at a 15 minute frequency, the first car from Grosvenor departing at 8.30 a.m. (Sundays 2 p.m.) and the last at 10.30 p.m. (Sundays 10 p.m.); from the G.W.R. Station the first car left at 9.15 a.m. and the last at 11 p.m., and Sunday departures from the Old Bridge were from 2.30 to 10.30 p.m. This was the only tramway constructed by the company, which, however, also ran several horse-bus routes.

## ELECTRIC TRAMWAYS.

Application was made in January, 1900, for powers to construct 18 miles of route on a 4 ft. gauge, but as all the Local Authorities objected, the scheme was rejected. In 1902, the Bath Electric Tram-

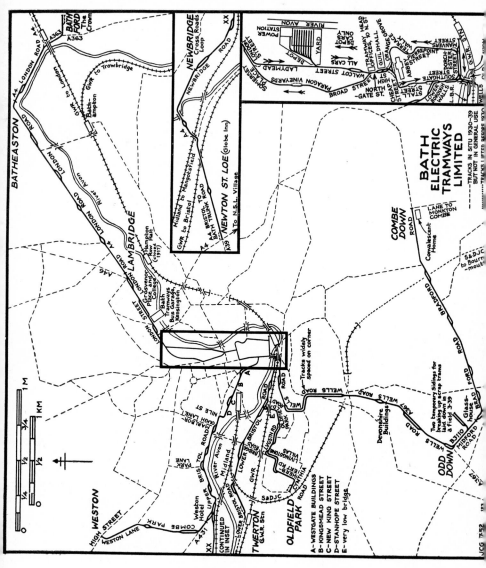

See also page 26.

ways, Ltd., was formed to " acquire, develop and work tramways in
or near Bath," and was registered on 9th July of that year.
This company duly purchased the horse tramway and commenced to
construct a fairly extensive electric system serving the city and out-

14

lying districts, the lines being held by the company in perpetuity.*
The horse-trams ceased operation on 25th July, 1902, and, the original
line having been reconstructed, the electric services were inaugurated
on 2nd January, 1904, over routes from Combe Down to Bathford,
G.W.R. Station to Weston and to Oldfield Park, and Guildhall to
Twerton. Cars at first used the track in Stall Street and Southgate
Street in both directions, but on 14th July, 1904, a line was opened
along Manvers Street and Pierrepont Street, forming a terminal loop
via Guildhall for Twerton and Oldfield Park cars. The opening
of the Newton St. Loe route on 5th August, 1905, completed the
system, which then had a total route mileage of 14.78. A small
reduction to 14.25 miles occurred in about 1918, when the Twerton
terminus was cut back from Messrs. Cook's clothing factory to the
former Twerton G.W.R. Station.

Several additional proposals for tramways and light railways in and
around Bath were mooted in the early years of this century, the
most important of which was a line between Bath and Bristol,
connecting with the respective systems at Newton St. Loe and Brislington. In later years a bus service was operated between Bristol
(Tramways Centre) and Newton St. Loe, through tickets being issued
from Bristol and Keynsham to Bath and vice versa, and it was not
until the early '30s that Bristol buses ran through to Bath. Powers
were actually obtained for an extension from Newton St. Loe to
Saltford (roughly halfway) but the scheme failed, as also did the
Bristol Company's extension from Brislington to Keynsham. A
proposed " Bath and Lansdown Light Railway " from Weston to the
Racecourse, partly rack-operated, also failed to come to fruition in
1905. There was also a plan to build a line from Kingsmead Square
to the Twerton route by way of the Midland Bridge, and the latter
structure was actually built with one tram track laid in place; this
was later removed.

The system was far from being an easy one to operate on account
of the steep gradients and narrow streets, but nevertheless it functioned
extremely well and during the whole of its life sustained only two
fatal accidents. The first of these occurred on the morning of 29th
May, 1918, when car No. 12 ran away out of control on the gradient
between Newbridge Road and the junction at the Weston Hotel,
where it jumped the track and overturned on to the pavement. One
passenger—a local councillor—was killed. The car was being driven

*From further information since received, it is understood that the
company's franchise was not in perpetuity as stated but only for a period
of 32 years, after which the local authority could exercise an option to
purchase the undertaking. On the abandonment of the tramways, these
rights were surrendered by the local authorities by agreement. The system
was built under the provisions of the Light Railways Act, 1896.

by one of the company's women employees at the time, and after this accident only male drivers were employed! The second mishap took place on the afternoon of Monday, 3rd July, 1933, when cars 18 and 6, bound for Glasshouse and Combe Down respectively, were ascending Wells Road. The leading car, No. 6, after stopping for an obstruction, failed to restart on the 1 in 14.4 gradient owing to tar having melted on to the rails. It ran back for 356 yards, under partial control, where it struck No. 18 and the two cars travelled together for a further 150 yards. Fortunately damage was confined to the platforms, and neither car was derailed, nor even did either trolley leave the wire. From the Ministry of Transport Inspector's report after the accident, it appears that the magnetic brakes were inclined to lock the wheels as they were interconnected, consequently the car slid for the greater part of the distance. Also it was not possible for the driver to apply sand at the conductor's end, although one car was so fitted. Two passengers lost their lives (one through jumping off the car), three were detained in hospital and six sent home after treatment.

The Bath tramways penetrated beyond the city limits to a large extent, for the Newton St. Loe, Bathford and Combe Down routes all reached into the country—particularly the Newton line, from which there was hardly a house to be seen all the way from Cross

*S. Miles Davey.*

Cars standing in the Walcot Street depot.

Double-deck car entering Pierrepont Street to reverse at G.W.R. station.
Note now only one track from Old Bridge to Pierrepont Street.

Roads Loop to the terminus. These routes, however, were well
patronised in the summer as the termini were good "jumping off
points" for country rambles, etc., and the Combe Down line, climbing
to a height of over 500 feet above sea level, afforded fine views of
the Cotswolds and as far as Salisbury Plain.

In December, 1936, control of the undertaking, together with its
bus-operating subsidiary, Bath Tramways Motor Co., Ltd., was
assumed by the Bristol Tramways & Carriage Co., Ltd., who
subsequently came to an agreement with the Bath City Council for
the replacement of the trams by Bristol-built buses. The first formal
announcement concerning the intended change-over was made by
Alderman A. W. Wills at a meeting of the City Council on 27th July,
1937, the day after he had concluded the agreement with the B.T.
& C. Co., Ltd., and the abandonment commenced in the following
year.

The first section to go was Newbridge Road terminus to Newton
St. Loe, which ceased operation on Saturday, 3rd November, 1938.
Its demise, however, was not without humour. What was supposedly
the last car to Newton St. Loe (No. 14) duly left the G.W.R. Station
at 10.55 p.m., but upon arrival at Cross Roads Loop, all passengers
were transferred to a bus, which ran them through to Newton. The
real "last tram" from Newton had departed some 30 minutes earlier,
much to the mortification of a small crowd of people which had
gathered at Newton to cheer the retiring vehicle on its way. Apparently

this was done deliberately to avoid the risk of scenes so up-
roarious as the Bristol Company had recently experienced on "last
tram nights!"

The next withdrawal was that of the Twerton route on Saturday
evening, 22nd April, 1939, and the rest of the system was closed
down in one fell swoop a fortnight later, 6th May.  During that day,
cars coming out of service were driven from the depot through the
city to a piece of waste land near Glasshouse, which had been selected
as the scrap yard.  The last cars from each terminus that night were
packed to capacity, and that from Bathford (No. 1) was followed by
a procession of motor cars.  Some 200 or more people waited at
Oldfield Park to see the last single-decker off on its journey to the
Guildhall, and on the Newbridge Road car a bottle of wine was
produced and healths drunk!  Fireworks accompanied the last car
from Weston.  The last of all, No. 22, from Combe Down, arrived
at the Guildhall about midnight, where it was met by the Mayor,
accompanied by members of the Corporation, Officials and the
General Manager of the company.  A dense crowd of well over a
thousand people cheered the car on its final journey to Walcot Depot

W. J. Haynes.
Single-deck car No. 54, one of the second batch, at Guildhall.

18

Double- and single-deck cars and replacing bus in Pierrepont Street.

with a hundred passengers on board, the Mayor at the controls, SPECIAL on the indicator, but strange to say, no decorations. The Mayor then switched off the power supply in Northgate Street to mark the occasion.

## SERVICES.

The system was worked as follows, the frequencies shown being those operative in 1933:

(i)  Combe Down—Guildhall—Bathford (Northbound via Manvers Street and the Paragon; southbound via Walcot Street and Southgate Street). Journey time, 48 minutes. Weekday frequencies: every 20 minutes until 11 a.m., then every 15 minutes, while on Sundays a 20 minute service was run in the morning and a 10 minute service in the afternoon until 5.30 p.m., then every 14 minutes. A high proportion of the workings were either Bathford to Glasshouse or Lambridge to Combe Down, and regular short workings were also run to Devonshire Buildings; a few cars also operated as far as Batheaston only at certain times.

(ii)  G.W.R. Station—Newton St. Loe. Journey time 24 minutes. Frequencies: weekdays 30 minutes, Saturday afternoons 12-20 minutes. Sundays a.m. 60 minutes, p.m. 30 minutes.

19

(iii)  G.W.R.  Station—Newbridge  Road.  Journey  time  17 minutes.  Frequencies: weekdays 15 minutes, Saturday afternoons 12 minutes, Sunday a.m. 20 minutes, p.m. 15 minutes.

(iv)  G.W.R.  Station—Weston.  Journey time 17 minutes.  Frequencies: weekdays 15 minutes, Saturday afternoons 12 minutes, Sunday a.m. 24 minutes, p.m. 15 minutes.  There was one short working to the Weston Hotel on Sunday mornings only.

(v)  Guildhall—Twerton  (outwards via Stall Street and inwards via Manvers Street).  Journey time 14 minutes.  Weekday service every 15 minutes until midday, then increased to every 10 minutes and 8 minutes on Saturday evenings.  Sunday service every 15 minutes until evening, then every 10 minutes.

(vi)  Guildhall—Oldfield Park (outwards via Stall Street, inwards via Manvers Street).  Journey time 14 minutes.  Weekday frequencies: mornings 15 minutes, afternoons 10 minutes, evenings 8 minutes until 8 p.m., then 10 minutes.  Saturday afternoons 7 minutes, evenings 6 minutes, Sunday mornings 20 minutes, afternoons 10 minutes.

## TICKETS.

This system was remarkable for the number of changes in ticket style and colour, no particular scheme being discernible in either design or colour.  At any one time, however, tickets were distinctively coloured.  3d. 5088, deep pink, shows an early (c.1910) full geographical ticket with no overprint.  1d. 7894, white with green overprint, shows later (c. 1919) straight across stage sections with fare overprinted.  1d. 0783, lilac with red overprint (Jan., 1924), has straight down stages and a different overprint.  1½d. transfer 1987 (May, 1927), white with red overprint has cancellation spaces on the back: in this instance the cancellation is a letter F.  2½d. return 1939, yellow (mid '30s), shows title at bottom and no overprint.  1d. transfer 4041, white with black overprint (late '20s), shows yet another style of transfer.  2d. 3095 blue, is the last type to be issued by the company.  2½d. 4041 shows the style in use after take over by Bristol and is based on that company's bus type.

For the Bath-Keynsham & Bristol joint service inaugurated January, 1927, Bath issued 7d. yellow, 2313, with red overprint and 9d. buff with red overprint and these tickets bore the names of both companies, with Bath first.  Passengers travelled by tram to Newton St. Loe and exchanged these tickets on the bus for an Exchange A, Newton St. Loe to Bristol, orange with black overprint, or Exchange B, 0274, Newton St. Loe to Keynsham, lilac with black overprint.  These exchange tickets bore the names of both companies, although purely Bristol territory, with Bristol leading.  In the reverse direction,

Bristol issued 9d. dull green from Bristol, 2221, and 7d. very dark blue from Keynsham, both with skeleton black overprint and with the names of both companies, and Bath issued an exchange, with their name only on it, in lilac with red overprint, on the tram from Newton St. Loe, 9764. This joint service did not last long and was succeeded by through Bristol-Bath buses.

### ROLLING STOCK.

The original fleet at the time of opening consisted of 26 open-top cars of the balcony type (Nos. 1-26) and four single-deckers (Nos. 50-53). Concurrently with the 1905 extension to Newton St. Loe, the company purchased ten more cars, these comprising eight open-top cars, which were numbered 27-34 and were identical with the original cars, and two more single-deckers, the latter being numbered 54 and 55 and differing from the earlier batch only in having rounded instead of square dash-boards. The fleet numbers 35-49 were presumably reserved for the purchase of further cars (possibly in connection with the intended extension to Saltford), but these did not materialise and the numbers were never used, the fleet remaining at the total of 40 cars throughout the life of the system.

All the car bodies were supplied by Milnes and were unvestibuled. The same firm supplied all the trucks which were of the 6 ft. wheelbase rigid type. Two 30 h.p. motors were fitted, and controllers were

S. Miles Davey.

No. 18 at Bathford terminus.

British Westinghouse with five series, three parallel and seven brake notches. Peacock quick-acting hand brakes actuated one cast iron block on each wheel, and there was a magnetic track brake connected by linkage to the wheel blocks so that when the magnetic brake was energised the resulting drag served to apply the brake blocks to all four wheels. There was, however, no automatic run-back preventer. Foot-operated sanding gear was provided, which sanded both rails in front of the leading wheels. There was also an arrangement for operating sanding valves when the magnetic brakes were applied, but except for one car, this only applied sand in front. Seating capacities were 55 on the double-deckers and 30 on the single-deckers. These latter cars provided the whole of the service on the Oldfield Park route, where their use was necessitated by a low clearance under the railway bridge in Lower Oldfield Park, but for many years up to about 1930, they were also to be seen on the adjacent Twerton route on weekday mornings; they have also been seen operating to Lambridge for the football matches (before Bath City F.C. moved to Twerton), but only ventured to other parts of the system on very rare occasions, and then only for some special reason.

There was in addition one water car, which carried no number and was seldom seen on the streets. One of the passenger cars (No. 10), however, was adapted for similar purposes and in this condition was shorn of its trolley standard, top-deck lights and indicators, and had the trolley pole protruding from the centre of the top-deck floor. This " pruning " treatment enabled it to operate to Oldfield Park, and it was the only double-decker to do so.

It is worth mentioning that car No. 21, in its later years, carried a roller-blind destination indicator behind the centre window of the saloon on each side. This was experimental and no others were so fitted. All cars originally had indicators fitted higher above the guard rails than latterly.

After abandonment, the whole of the stock was broken up, many of the cars being burnt in the scrap yard at Glasshouse. As if to act as a memorial to this sad event, one of the tram stop signs remained in place in Midford Road, only a short distance away, for some years.*

### LIVERY.

*Very Bright Blue.* Cant rail, waist panel, dash and stair bands. Lined in white. Number in gold shaded pink.

*Primrose Yellow.* Upper deck panelling, window frames, rocker panel and bulkhead. Black outer line and blue inner line on rocker

*The tram stop sign was still in place in June, 1952.

23

panel. Title on rocker panel in gold shaded blue. Upper deck panels lined blue only. Stair risers yellow and black.

*White.* Inside of dash. Controller black.

*Light Oxide Brown.* Truck, lifeguard tray, handrails and iron scrollwork at corner of dash.

*Dark Blue.* Destination box, platform step, trolley mast and lifeguard gate.

*Aluminium Paint.* Wire netting round upper deck. In the earlier days, cars had a gold monogram on the waist panel.

*H. B. Priestley, B.Sc.*
Nos. 8 and 9 in the depot.
No. 53, one of the original single-deck cars at Guildhall.

24

# TRACK.

Measured as single line, the track originally totalled 18.68 miles, but the slight curtailment at Twerton and the removal of double line junctions at Walcot Church and the G.W.R. Station, also of several superfluous loops (see map), reduced the total to 18.25 miles. During the 'twenties, however, three loops on the Combe Down line and one at Grosvenor Place were lengthened in order to reduce waiting time and so speed up the service. The rails used weighed 95 lb. per yard and were laid to the 4 ft. 8½ in. gauge. The only appreciable stretch of double track was that in Wells Road, which was about ¾ mile long and included the steepest gradient on the system, 1 in 10.7. The single line in Nile Street (Weston-Newton route), having a blind corner at each end, was protected by colour light signals; red lamp signals were also installed outside the Depot and the Tramway Offices in Northgate Street, but these were indications or instructions to drivers rather than traffic control signals. The sharpest curvature had a 38 ft. radius, and there was no reserved track. The Newton St. Loe, Oldfield Park and Bathford termini had a double track lay-out, but the second track was later removed in each case, and thereafter the Bath system became notable for the long stretch of single line with which its routes ended. Most of the loops gave a straight run in.

## CURRENT COLLECTION.

Overhead trolley with swivelling head and suspension mainly by means of side poles and brackets. The bracket arms on some sections—notably Bathford—were of unusual length. Automatic trolley reversers were installed at the termini but not at the intermediate reversing points nor at the G.W.R. Station. Frogs were of the drop-arm type. Wires were provided for running in both directions in Southgate Street and the junction at Old Bridge was fully wired. Trolleys were turned by ropes at the intermediate points, and the single deckers carried a bamboo pole, though this was only needed when leaving the depot or in case of dewirement.

## DEPOT.

This was located at Walcot Street and housed the entire fleet on eight roads. Cars proceeding from Guildhall to the depot ran direct up Walcot Street against the normal one-way rule. The premises are now used as a factory. The scrap yard laid out at Glasshouse in 1939 had two tracks laid into an old quarry working between St. Martin's Hospital and Glasshouse corner. The site has since been built over.

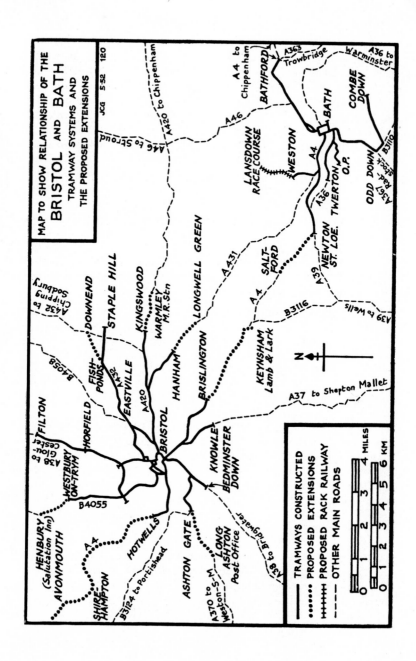

MAP TO SHOW RELATIONSHIP OF THE
**BRISTOL** AND **BATH**
TRAMWAY SYSTEMS AND
THE PROPOSED EXTENSIONS

JCG 5·52 120

TRAMWAYS CONSTRUCTED
PROPOSED EXTENSIONS
PROPOSED RACK RAILWAY
OTHER MAIN ROADS

# BRISTOL

## HORSE TRAMWAYS.

The first enactment for the construction of tramways in Bristol was granted to the Bristol Corporation in 1872 in respect of a line, 1 mile 62 chains in length, extending from The King David Inn in Perry Road via Queens Road and Whiteladies Road to St. John's Church, Redland, at the foot of Blackboy Hill. Work on the line commenced in 1873 and the above section was completed in the following spring, but the Corporation were not empowered to work the tramway. The Bristol Tramways Co., Ltd., was therefore formed for the purpose of doing so under lease. The rent to be paid by the company was fixed at a nominal amount for the first five years, £360 per annum for the next three years, £480 for the next three and £600 for the remainder of the 21-year term. The line cost £14,000 to build, and was opened on 9th August, 1875.

The 'Western Daily Press' of 10th August, 1875, has recorded that "At twelve o'clock the Mayor and several members of the Corporation with others, in compliance with an invitation issued by the directors, were in Perry Road and took their seats in the cars. Each car was drawn by four splendid horses in new harness. The uniform of the drivers and conductors is of a greyish colour with scarlet trimmings. Everything being ready, the whistle was sounded and the cars started the journey, the course being kept clear by the police under Supt. Thatcher of the Clifton Division. All along the route crowds of people had assembled and as the cars passed, hearty cheers were offered for the success of the tramways."

The company thereupon proceeded with the construction of further routes, and on 4th December, 1875, an extension from Perry Road down Colston Street to St. Augustine's Parade (subsequently to be known as The Tramways Centre) was brought into use, as had been planned by the Corporation originally. This was followed by a line from Old Market Street to Eastville in June, 1876. In September, 1876, the latter route was linked with the original Redland line by way of Broadmead and The Horsefair and a through service instituted between Eastville and Blackboy Hill. A tram service from Old Market to St. George (church) was inaugurated in October, 1876,

27

The first horse tram at Perry Road curve, then the terminus, on inaugural trip.

despite a vigorous protest from owners and occupiers of shop property along the route. Work was also put in hand on a line from Bristol Bridge to Totterdown (The Three Lamps) which was opened as far as Bath Bridge in April, 1879, and completed in November of the same year.

Three further routes were opened during the year 1880, namely to Hotwells (Dowry Square) on 24th June; to Bedminster on 17th November; and Horfield (Egerton Road) on 18th November. The lines built in the 'seventies were laid on Joseph Kincaid's system, and this engineer's improved system, employing 50 lb. per yard rails of wedge-shape section laid in cast iron chairs, was used in the 1880 extensions; its cost amounted to £4,023 15s. per mile single line. The company's returns for the year ended 30th June, 1880, were as follows*:

| | | |
|---|---|---|
| Gross receipts | ... | £27,028. |
| Working expenses | ... | £20,885. |
| Net profit | ... | £6,173. |
| Passengers carried | ... | 3,689,169. |
| Car miles run | ... | 500,873 |
| Mileage open | ... | 9 miles 25 chains. |
| Rolling stock | ... | 53 cars and 228 horses. |

Owing to severe gradients, it had been decided to work the Horfield section by steam power and seven locomotives of the conventional

*D. K. Clarke: ' Tramways, their construction and working,' Vol. 11, 1881.

enclosed type were obtained from the Hughes Engine Co., Ltd., under a 12 months' contract. A contemporary photograph shows locomotive No. 6, named "Loughborough," doubtless in honour of Messrs. Hughes' place of business, coupled to an early horse car which had been fitted with a crude awning over the top deck, the locomotive chimney being extended horizontally backwards into another chimney fitted to the front of the car so as to discharge its smoke and fumes above "roof" level! This, together with any other horse cars which may have been similarly embellished for steam operation, would almost certainly have been the only top-covered trams to run in Bristol.

The inauguration of the steam trams was accompanied by much public ceremony. The 'Daily Press' of 19th November, 1880, says that a great crowd of citizens assembled in the Horsefair when the directors of the company, members of the Corporation, members of the Horfield Local Board and others took their seats for the first run over the new line. A writer in 1925 says he well remembers standing at the rails of the school house in Stokes Croft to watch the gaily decorated cars pass. There was (as usual) a luncheon afterwards and Mr. J. C. Wall, on proposing "success to the Tramway Company," opened his speech with the remark "I must admit if it had been left to me you would never have had a Tramway Company in Bristol." The sturdy old Alderman was one of the most bitter opponents of trams of any sort, but apparently he had overcome his

B.T. & C. Co., Ltd.

Trace horses being attached to car on the Hotwells route just after leaving "The Drawbridge."

*Block and photo 'Bristol Observer.'*

Steam tram engine "Loughborough" and trailer. Note top-deck canopy and chimney extension.

scruples by the time steam trams were introduced. These engines were refuelled and watered under what is now the Gospel Hall. It was said to be " a messy affair."

In addition to the Hughes' engines, there was also one built by the local firm of Fox, Walker & Co., which was a rather shorter and squarer engine painted white. This engine was used on the Eastville to Redland route and used to experience some difficulty negotiating the Infirmary Hill. The steam cars started from the Horsefair and were shedded in a small depot in Whitsun Street, St. Paul's.* They proved, however, to be neither popular nor economical and the contract was not renewed; the locomotives were returned to the makers and the service was taken over by horses. The last steam tram ran in November, 1881.

With the purpose of linking up all the inner termini on what had now become an extensive system, two connecting lines were opened in April, 1881, one from Bristol Bridge to Old Market via St. Philip's Bridge, and the other from Bristol Bridge to St. Augustine's Parade (The Drawbridge) via the newly widened Baldwin Street. In 1882, the company purchased the Redland line outright from the corporation, but this deal was only concluded after much negotiation. The line had been valued by the Municipal advisers at £10,000, but the company offered only £4,000. They were, however, seeking the corporation's consent to further extensions and one of the conditions attaching to this was the purchase of the Redland line at £8,000. The company were, therefore, obliged to pay that sum. On 1st January, 1888, it became amalgamated with a concern operating horse cabs (The Bristol Carriage Co.) to form The Bristol Tramways and Carriage Co., Ltd. This event coincided with the opening of a further connecting line, namely from the Horsefair to St. Augustine's Parade, thus enabling Horfield cars to be worked into the Tramways Centre.

Expansion of the horse car system continued in Bristol until a considerably later date than in most places, and a final batch of extensions opened during the 'nineties consisted of the following sections:

St. George to Kingswood, Stokes Croft to Ashley Road, and Horfield (Egerton Road) to Horfield Depot, all in 1892. Bedminster (Cannon Street) to Ashton Gate in 1896; and Ashley Road to Stapleton Road and Three Lamps to Arnos Vale, both in 1898.

The published returns for 1881 showed that the company was then operating 70 double-deck horse cars and 300 horses, but subsequent additions brought the stock to 85 cars. The early ones had six windows per side and seated 16 passengers on each deck, with knife-board seating outside and open-rung spiral iron stairs,

*Absorbed into a bus station in 1958/9.

but the later cars were longer, having seven side windows, and had transverse " garden " seats and more substantial side protection on the upper deck. The fleet also included a single-deck toastrack type, of which there are believed to have been four. A further batch of horse cars numbered 98-115 was purchased for the extensions opened between 1892 and 1898 and some of these were used as trailers behind electric cars on the Kingswood route in its early years. Five horses were required to draw a car up Infirmary Hill, and four up Colston Street and College Green, while three were required on several other steep stretches. The depots were later used for electric cars (*vide infra*) except those in Colston Street and Victoria Street. The former premises became the headquarters of the outside Electrical Department, and much later a G.P.O. garage. It was never wired for electric cars. It is still complete with wrought iron gates bearing the monogram of the company, and the monogram, in stone, of the original Bristol Tramways Co., can also be seen. The Victoria Street premises were converted into a tramway station to serve Temple Meads railway station, and a good deal of spare trackage in the yard can still be seen from the station approach. The principal stables for the horses were situated in Old Market Street and comprised three decks.

*' Tramway & Railway World.'*
Electric car with horse trailer at St. George Fountain on Kingswood route soon after the opening. Note peculiar trolley head. The destination names are painted on the sides of both cars.

# ELECTRIC TRAMWAYS.

At one time the Bristol Tramways and Carriage Co., Ltd., was associated with the Imperial Tramways Company, whose headquarters were in Bristol and whose Chairman was Sir James Clifton Robinson, the well-known pioneer of electric traction. Largely through this influence, Bristol became among the first cities in the British Isles to have electric tramways on the overhead trolley system. The Old Market—Kingswood line, but lately the subject of a horse-car extension, was equipped for electric operation, and opened on 14th October, 1895, accompanied by the usual banquet and speeches. The first car to Kingswood was No. 89. The 22 motor cars and sundry horse-cars used as trailers then in service carried 30,000 passengers on August Bank Holiday, 1896.

The Old Market—Eastville route was electrified as from 1st February, 1897, and extended to Fishponds in September and to Staple Hill in November of the same year. By 11th June, 1899*, electric cars were running between Old Market and Bristol Bridge, and from the Tramways Centre to Arnos Vale, where the new works and depot were opened. Shortly afterwards the electrification of the whole of the remaining system was put in hand, and all routes were working by electric traction on 2nd December, 1900, including extensions to Horfield Barracks, Bedminster Down, Knowle, Brislington, Durdham Downs via Redland Green and to Hanham; powers for the last-named extension were obtained on 28th November, 1898, under the Light Railways Act of 1896 and the line was known officially as The St. George and Hanham Light Railway†. A short connecting line was opened along Barrs Street on 28th March, 1901, enabling cars from Old Market to reach Zetland Road.

A further Act of Parliament passed in 1904 gave the company powers to construct the following extensions:

1.—From Blackboy Hill across the Downs by the Westbury Road, through Westbury to The Salutation Inn, Henbury.

2.—From the existing terminus at Horfield Barracks to Filton, terminating in the heart of the village.

3.—From the " Cross Hands " at Fishponds to Downend.

4.—From the existing Kingswood terminus down Warmley Hill to Warmley Station.

---

*Some accounts say July.

†There was a clause compelling them to paint the posts, standards and brackets once a year with a colour approved by the Local Authority. Provision was also to be made to allow the Local Authority to use the posts for public lamps. Display of advertisements on posts was prohibited. The County Council also asked for the suspension of working on the occasion of public demonstrations, but this was not granted.

33

5.—From the existing Hanham terminus along the main road to Longwells Green.

6.—From the existing terminus at Brislington along the main Bath Road to Keynsham, and terminating at the end of High Street at the junction of the roads opposite " The Lamb and Lark."

7.—From the existing terminus at Ashton railway bridge along the main Weston Road through Long Ashton, and terminating near the Post Office.

The above extensions represented a route length of about 12 miles. Only one fully materialised, however, namely that from Horfield Barracks to Filton, which was opened in March, 1907, and one was partly built, namely the Downs-Westbury section of the Henbury extension. This was opened in 1908 and was the last tramway construction to be carried out in Bristol. The final route and track mileages were 31.10 and 58.83 miles respectively. In the early 'twenties, when The Portway was being built alongside the River Avon from Hotwells to Avonmouth, and the Bristol Port and Pier Railway was closed, a proposal was made for a high-speed tramway, and conduits for the cables were actually laid in, but in view of the Corporation's opposition the plan was not proceeded with.

There is no doubt that when at its zenith, the Bristol tramway system was widely regarded as a model undertaking from the viewpoint of efficiency and maintenance. There was also a great spirit of loyalty between the employees and the company; for instance, the signal box at Colston Street was not electrified, as it would have meant that a faithful old servant of the company would be without work. The company also had turned its attention to buses as feeders to the tram routes at an early date, for the first was established in 1877 to feed the trams at St. George. In 1881 a service of omnibuses was opened between the Drawbridge and the Suspension Bridge, and in 1900 buses were running between the Station and Long Ashton. Motor omnibuses were introduced in 1906 and services were run to Thornbury and Saltford. Although these were used extensively as feeder services, the tramways themselves catered for the bulk of the traffic very satisfactorily. For instance, ' The Evening Times and Echo ' of 7th July, 1913, reporting on the handling of the traffic at the Royal Show then being held on The Downs, states that 225 tram cars, 42 motor charabancs of various types, 230 taxicabs, private landaulets and torpedo-cars and 150 horses were employed. The tram cars and motor-charabancs alone carried during the week ended 5th July, 1,560,428 passengers, and on the Clifton Rocks Railway, 14,300 passengers were carried. After comparing conditions with the Royal Show of 1878, when the horse-car route to the foot of the Blackboy Hill was greatly overloaded, it goes on to say: " How changed are the conditions at The Downs now, with a terminus superior to any in the Kingdom to favour the quick despatch of cars. With the two sets of rails leading to Upper Belgrave Road and the one set leading towards Stoke Road, these constitute a triple terminus, and a dozen cars can be loading or unloading at one time. Then there is the additional terminus at the Westbury Road junction not far away. 12 additional men were employed on each show day at the Durdham Downs terminus to assist in the loading of the cars. The passengers, by means of printed notices on the cars, were requested to leave at the front end, and new passengers were admitted only at the rear end. . . . Time after time a car arrived with from 50 to 70 passengers in it, was unloaded and by the time the last passenger had passed out of the front end all the seats were again filled, with some standing, and the car sent away again within 90 seconds of arrival. Over 80 cars were employed on the three steeply graded routes leading to the Downs which put a severe test on the capabilities of the generators, but there were no breakdowns." Details are given of the despatch of cars, over 40 being sent away in 30 minutes, which did not include those on the regular five minute Westbury service. Allowing 70 passengers per outward car and 50 per inward car, it is computed that the trams dealt with passengers at the rate of 9,600 per hour. The electric trams took 16 minutes to cover the two miles to the Centre, whereas the horse cars had taken 24 minutes from only the bottom of Blackboy Hill.

During the whole history of the company there was only one accident, which was in 1901, when a car ran away on Blackboy Hill and overturned, seriously injuring the driver.

Under the Tramways Act, 1870, the Bristol Corporation could claim the option of purchasing the tramways from the company in 1915, but due largely to the war conditions then prevailing, they decided not to proceed in this direction although the necessary powers for municipal operation had been obtained in the previous year. Under a further provision of the Act, the city's option recurred every seven years, and it was not until the third recurrence, in 1936, that the Corporation finally decided to exercise it. By this time, however, the company had built up an extensive network of motor bus services, not only in Bristol itself, but throughout the neighbouring counties, having opened branches at Bath, Weston-super-Mare, Cheltenham, Gloucester, Wells and Swindon. With this in view, a joint working agreement between the two parties was drawn up in respect of the Bristol City services. This provided for the purchase of the tramways by the Corporation at a cost of £1,125,000 on 1st October, 1937, and the conversion of the system to motor bus operation within the next two years; the city services to be jointly owned by the company. Trolleybuses were never seriously considered, though the company had built two such vehicles. These were sold to Pontypridd and Doncaster. It is rumoured that one was tested in Victoria Street at night, using a skate as earth on the tram line.

The abandonment of the tramways commenced on 8th May, 1938, with the withdrawal of the Hotwells and Westbury services and the Durdham Downs—Eastville service, followed on 3rd September, of the same year by the Staple Hill, Brislington and Knowle routes. The Hanham—Knowle cross-city service was then cut back to Old Market Street, and the track between Bristol Bridge and Old Market ceased to be used, though it was kept in working order. The next stage of the programme took place on 15th July, 1939, when the Filton and Downs via Zetland Road routes were abandoned, and the Centre—Kingswood service curtailed at Old Market, the track between there and the Centre being closed. The 'Bristol Evening Post' of 17th July, 1939, records the passing of the last tram from The Tramway Centre in the following words: " The last trams to run on The Centre—Durdham Downs and Centre—Filton routes faded quietly from their duties on Saturday evening, and now their place is taken by motor buses. Bidding ' good bye ' to the ' last tram ' has of late tended to become a somewhat hectic event (a reference to the closure of the Brislington route which was attended by much hooliganism and no little looting) but special precautions were taken on this occasion to ensure comfort and safety, and nowhere was there any untoward scene. At the Centre a large crowd of people assembled late in the evening to give the last tram a cheery send-off, but there was some doubt as to which was really the last tram. Eventually when a tram moved off with an Ashley Down Road sign and three police officers on board, the crowd realised that this was the last chapter of tram history at The Centre, and people scrambled to get on board. The police saw to it, however, that the tram had the permitted number of passengers and no more. People ran alongside it as it moved along Colston Avenue. Apparently the excitement was too much for the old tram, for it broke down after about 50 yards (apparently only a dewirement). While two tramway men made a quick repair to the conductor arm at the top of the tram, the crowd surged round and Press photographers took pictures of the veteran making the last journey. As soon as the repair was complete, the tram moved off briskly, followed by a long line of motor cars and cycles, and there was a large crowd when the procession arrived in grand style at the Ashley Down Road depot at Horfield. Some of the crowd cheered and sang ' Auld Lang Syne ' as the vehicle trundled slowly into the depot. In all about 50 trams were taken out of service without any incident of note."

*B.T. & Co., Ltd.*

Bedminster depot on the morning of 4th January, 1941.

The four remaining routes—Kingswood, Hanham, Ashton Gate and Bedminster Down—were scheduled for change-over in the following October, but the outbreak of war in September and the resulting fuel restrictions caused this final abandonment to be postponed. The company later resolved to complete the change-over, but when the end finally did come, it was brought about largely by enemy action. On the night of 3rd January, 1941, a corner of Bedminster depot was demolished by a high-explosive bomb, and much of the rolling stock therein destroyed or damaged. No. 71 was flung on its side and completely wrecked; No. 164 had one platform and the dash-board smashed; the others suffered mainly by broken windows. No. 9 had been abandoned earlier on in West Street and a H.E. dropped in front of it, flinging it against a butcher's shop and completely wrecking it; No. 26 nearby had its windows smashed. In any case, as the bomb fell at the entrance, it would have been impossible to get any of the cars out. Recent breaking up of stock having left only enough for bare requirements, the Bedminster and Ashton routes had to be taken over by buses. The cars from Bedminster depot were driven to Kingswood (except for a short stretch in Bath Street and Tower Hill where the overhead was down and they were towed by a lorry) and soon afterwards broken up there. Nos. 15 and 105 which were undamaged, having been at Ashton Gate terminus were put into service on the Kingswood route. Then, on 11th April of the same year, the Kingswood and Hanham routes were abruptly discontinued upon the severance by a bomb of the main current supply from the St. Philip's Bridge power house at Counterslip. The old generating station at St. George was not able to supply enough power, and after

Photo: ' Bristol Evening World,' block: F. G. Warne, Ltd.
No. 9 destroyed by enemy action in West Street, Bedminster.

some opposition from the Ministry concerned had been overcome, bus operation of these routes became permanent and all the remaining trams were broken up.

Although now entirely a bus operator, the company still keeps the title it adopted 60 years ago, despite the fact that it has dispensed with both "Tramways" and "Carriages."* Having developed the Motor Constructional Works at Brislington, where it manufactures buses not only for itself but for other undertakings, the company was the only British tramway operator to enter the commercial vehicle market, and it was also closely associated with the Bristol Aeroplane

*It became Bristol Omnibus Co. on 31st May, 1957.

Company in the latter's early days. The company also ran the Clifton Rocks Railway (see anon) and purchased the Bath and Weston-super-Mare tramway systems for replacement by its own buses. Another undertaking with which the company was connected was the Corris Railway, a Welsh narrow-gauge line which was owned by the Imperial Tramway Company at one time.* It is a widely held impression that this railway was actually owned by Bristol Tramways, but this is incorrect as the association was purely one of common control by the Imperial Tramways Company, who, incidentally, also ran the Middlesbrough, Stockton and Thornaby Tramways. The operating and manufacturing side of the Bristol Tramways & Carriage Co., Ltd., was latterly controlled by the Tilling organisation, which recently sold its transport interests to the British Transport Commission.

Between 1929 and 1931, 60% of the shares in the company were held by the Great Western Railway, but this fact was never published as the railway company had no powers to run tramways. Their interest passed to the Western National Omnibus Co., Ltd.

### SERVICES.

The electric services followed very closely the routes operated by the horse cars, and were operated as under, service numbers being introduced in December, 1913:

1. Centre—Whiteladies Road—Durdham Downs.
2. Centre—Durdham Downs—Westbury.
3. Eastville—Old Market—Durdham Downs.
4. Centre—Zetland Road—Durdham Downs.
5. Centre—Gloucester Road—Horfield Barracks.
6. Centre—Horfield—Filton.
7. Centre—City Road—Eastville—Fishponds.
8. Centre—Temple Meads Station.
9. Brislington—Centre—Hotwells.
10. Bristol Bridge—Knowle.
11. Bristol Bridge—Ashton Gate.
12. Bristol Bridge—Bedminster Down.
13. Old Market—St. George—Kingswood.
14. Staple Hill—Old Market—Zetland Road Junction.
15. Hanham—Old Market—Bushey Park.
16. Old Market—St. George.
17. Temple Meads Station—Centre—Hotwells.

From about 1925 onwards the route numbers were dispensed with and services 1, 5, 8, 16, 17 withdrawn and replaced by strengthening

*The Imperial Tramways sold 12 to the Great Western Railway for a nominal sum.

the overlapping services. At the same time, service 13 was extended from Old Market to the Centre and service 15 from Bushey Park to Knowle. Short workings were put on between Centre and Filton Park, Centre and Eastville via City Road, Brislington Depot and Centre, Old Market and Whiteway Road and Marling Road, Staple Hill and Old Market, and Knowle to Nags Head Hill Top. Through services were also operated to Ashton Gate for football matches, and to the Downs for special occasions.

A parcels service by special delivery tram was once proposed but it was felt that this would interfere with passenger services and the scheme was never instituted.

### FARES AND TICKETS.

The original fares were arranged in penny stages to a maximum of fourpence. A penny in those days would take one from the Centre to Hotwells and even as far as from Bristol Bridge to Bedminster or Ashton! There was only one fourpenny ride, that being from Zetland Road to Staple Hill (route 14).

Then, in 1918, the minimum fare became 1½d. and a halfpenny was added to other values. That lasted until 1925, when penny fares returned, but with shorter stages than before.

Little is known of the tickets issued on the horse trams. During the electric era a systematic colour scheme was adhered to with few exceptions. This was 1d. blue, 2d. white, 3d. pink, and 4d. green. During the 1914-18 war increases, ½d. values were introduced and the penny fare was raised to 1½d., retaining the same colour: additional values took the colours 1½d. salmon (on reversion of the penny to blue), 2½d. yellow, 3½d. lilac, 4½d. buff, 5d. and 5½d. grey. Children's tickets were originally all white, but about 1930 became 1d. grass green, 1½d. reddish brown, and 2d. white. Workmen's tickets were in early days 2d. lilac or orange, 3d. grey and 4d. yellow. Tickets giving transfer facilities were 3d. white and 3½d. nile green. In the '30s, workmen's tickets were the same as ordinary tickets with the addition of red stripes on the edges, and later down the middle. A ½d. buff workman's single was in issue at one time. Full geographical tickets were issued till 1917/18 (1d. 4041, and the through tram—rocks railway 3d. 9884). For a few years at the end of the '14-'18 war number type tickets were issued (2d. 9927). With the stabilisation of fares, names were again introduced together with overprints and the tickets were lettered according to the route(s) served (1½d. 0480); on the higher values several routes were combined on one ticket. It should be noted that the company's name now appears on the bottom of the ticket. In the late '30s there was a change of printers and the initials of the company only are printed, this time at the top (1d.

workmen's return 3694). Finally when portions of certain routes were being operated by buses, bus type tickets with tram transfer facilities were issued (2½d. 2771).

1d. Workman Single and 1d. Wounded Soldier.

## ROLLING STOCK.

The Bristol trams were all of the uncanopied open-top single-truck type and remained so throughout the existence of the system, this being (except in its earlier years) by far the largest tram fleet in this country to be entirely made up of open-topped cars. That improvements were not made was due to the uncertain position created for the company by the Corporation's repeated postponement of their decision whether or not to acquire the system, circumstances under which the company not unnaturally felt disinclined to spend large sums of money on new or modernised stock. Bogie and covered-top cars were once envisaged but the plans were turned down by the manager for the reasons stated above. The situation was to some extent alleviated by an exceptionally high standard of maintenance. The design of the cars was very closely standardised and incorporated four arched-top windows per side, seating for 53 passengers, double bulkhead doors, and very shallow dashes, outside hand-brake columns the headlamps mounted at mid-deck position. Only the first 15 cars differed to any great extent, as will be shown later. Interior seating comprised upholstered longitudinal benches, while the outside seats were of the wooden " garden " pattern with a patent cover to keep the seat dry in wet weather. Wire mesh lifeguards were used instead of the usual wooden slat pattern.

Route indication in the earliest days followed the horse-tram custom of having the place names painted on the sides of the cars, but later Mr. Charles Challenger, the then Traffic Manager of the Bristol Tramways & Carriage Co., Ltd., introduced destination indicators on which both termini were displayed on rectangular plates made to slide into the front of the box, which was fixed above the guard rails

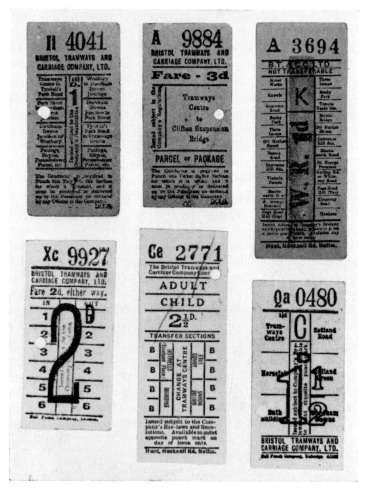

Early 1d. Workman's single for any distance beyond 1d. ordinary stage—white with green stripe.  Bristol Bridge terminus of Knowle route was at Morley Statue—this was removed when the line was moved to kerbside loading. 1d. Wounded Soldier ticket.  Grey with red figure—first issued 20th October, 1916.  Note similarity to current L.G.O.C. tickets.

and embellished with fancy wrought-iron scrollwork. The indicators were modified in 1913/14 before the introduction of service numbers and in 1925 the sliding plates were replaced by roller blinds showing only the destination, with one intermediate point where necessary; with the latter modification, the ironwork decoration was removed. A route board was also carried below the windows on each side, the line of direction being indicated by " hands " at each end.

A multi-aspect circular indicator was also carried above the bulk-head, displaying one of several colours to distinguish routes at night,

*' Tramway & Railway World.'*
View showing the " new " destination box. Part of the route name can be seen on the side. The resistances can also be seen under the platform.

and also to show the legal red indication at the rear. All cars were fitted with mechanical track brakes in view of the many steep hills, and there were a number of Board of Trade stops at the top of steep hills where the car had to be stopped dead and the wheel operating this brake applied. The wheelbase of nearly all cars was lengthened from 1920 onwards from 6 ft. to 6 ft. 6 in., all the trucks used having semi-elliptic springs. Experimental use was made of Mountain & Gibson and E.M.B. trucks at various times, the most sensational effort being car No. 87, which was fitted with a modern 7 ft. E.M.B. truck with magnetic brakes; this, however, proved to be unsatisfactory on sharp curves.

Details of cars constructed up to 1900 are as under:

(1-85 and 98-115 were the original horse cars.)

| | |
|---|---|
| 86– 97<br>116–118 | Built by American Car Co., 1895/6. Three side windows; seats 25/18 (later 29/24); Peckham trucks; G.E. 800 motors, 18 h.p. (later G.E. 58); K.2. controllers; single bulkhead doors, overall length 24 ft.; wheelbase 5 ft. 6 in., height to top of trolley standard 15 ft. 6 in. |
| 125–141 | Built by American Car Co., 1897/8. Four side windows; seats 29/24; Peckham trucks; G.E. 800 motors, 18 h.p. (later G.E. 58); K.2. controllers; No. 128 was later fitted with Peckham Pendulum truck. No. 141 had five side windows and was fitted out as the Manager's saloon, having individual bucket seats and all metal work plated. It was last used as such at the opening of the Westbury extension in 1908 and was shortly afterwards rebuilt as a standard car for normal service. |
| 142–161 | Built by American Car Co., 1899; four side windows; seats 29/24; Brill 21E trucks; G.E. 52 motors, 27 h.p. (later G.E. 58); K.10 controllers. Eight cars later fitted with Peckham trucks. |
| 1– 85<br>98–115<br>119–124<br>162–202 | Built by Milnes, Birkenhead, 1900; four side windows; seats 29/24; Peckham trucks; G.E. 58 motors, 30 h.p.; B.18 controllers. Car No. 7 later fitted with E.M.B. truck, and No. 13 with a Brill 21E truck. |
| 203–232 | Built by Milnes, Birkenhead, 1900; four side windows; seats 29/24; McGuire trucks; B.49 motors, 30 h.p.; B.90 controllers. Later alterations: 22 cars fitted with G.E.58 motors, 24 cars with Peckham trucks and six with Brill 21E trucks (including No. 203 and 213). |

*S. Miles Davey.*
Top deck seating showing tip-over covers to seats.

The composition of the fleet remained unchanged until 1920 when car 86 was scrapped and six new cars built. The latter were of the standard design and were constructed in the company's own works, their equipment comprising G.E.58 motors, B.18 controllers and Peck-

*S. Miles Davey.*
One of the rail grinders.

45

Platform view.

*S. Miles Davey.*

Lower saloon seating.  Note curtains.

ham trucks; these cars were numbered 86 (in replacement of the car
withdrawn) and 233-237, bringing the stock to its maximum total
of 237 cars.   Three cars (Nos. 92, 116 and 117) were withdrawn in
1923, and No. 97 in 1929, so that from then until abandonment
commenced in 1938 there were 233 cars in service.

In addition to the foregoing, there were four non-passenger cars.
Two of these were snow sweepers fitted with brushes and numbered
1 and 2, the latter being somewhat smaller than No. 1.   The regular
driver of one of them for many years was the late Mr. L. J. White,
who, 'tis said, was often sent for late on a winter's night just when
he was preparing to go to bed!   The other two were rail grinders
converted from cars 86 and 97 on their withdrawal from passenger
service, and in this later state they boasted canopies over the platforms
—a refinement which the company never afforded its passenger cars!

During and after abandonment all cars were broken up and the parts
burnt or sold as scrap.   There was a suggestion that one be preserved,
but this did not materialise.*

*A model, built about 1906, is preserved in the city museum.

## LIVERY.

Dark blue and white with gold lining on blue and blue lining on white parts, and large block-shaded numbers. These numbers were later reduced in size and simplified. The name of the company was also painted in large letters along the rocker panel until about 1925, when, as cars came in for repainting, it was replaced by small letters at the rear end only on each side. The special car, No. 141, was painted light blue until refitted for passenger service.

*Dark Blue.* (Navy tending to fade to a dull blue.) Waist panel, dash, stair bands and headlamp, sand box. Lined gold and white. (Gold latterly replaced by yellow.)

*White.* Cant rail, window frames, rocker panel and bulkhead. Rocker panel lined brown, cant rail lined blue. Title in brown letters shaded red on rocker panel.

*Red.* Corner posts, lined white. Shading to numbers and lettering.

*Orange.* Inside dash, controller and stair risers. Number on inside of dash in white shaded red. U/D seats.

*S. Miles Davey.*

Two cars at Kingswood terminus showing destination blacked out for security, bumper painted white, side and rear lights fitted low down and sand box painted white. The scrapping sidings are over the wall.

*Oxide Brown.* Wire netting round upper deck, trolley mast and handrails.

*Dull Blue.* Truck, lifeguards, platform step and destination box. In later years, the large title on the rocker panel was replaced by a title in small brown letters in the right-hand corner. The number on the dash was reduced in size. Route boards under the windows were in different colours.

*From an early postcard.*
Front view showing route numbers in use. Note the bold number on the front, the company's name in large letters on the rocker panel, and the circular indicator for displaying a coloured light at night, also the licence plate over the door.

This was laid to the standard gauge and consisted of grooved rails weighing 92½ lb. per yard, with welded fishplates and special bonding joints. Double track was laid from Perry Road to the bottom of Westbury Hill, Stokes Croft to Charborough Road, Old Market to St. George (except two short single line stretches near Lawrence Hill), Warwick Road junction to near Fishponds, and Fishponds to Staple Hill terminus; also on the Hotwells and Brislington routes throughout except for a short length of single track near Brislington terminus. The double track sections included several which were originally single or interlaced until the roads were widened. Facing or trailing crossovers were installed at regular intervals. The remainder of the system was single with passing loops, although many of the latter were quite long, and there was also a considerable amount of interlaced track, particularly in Stapleton Road.

The company showed considerable enterprise in the provision of special track layouts for specific purposes. In addition to an elaborate terminal layout arranged around a central triangular island at the

*C. F. Klapper.*

The centre loading island at the Tramways Centre. Cars to Horsefair on left, to Brislington on right and to Durdham Downs in foreground.

Tramways Centre, there was a similar but enlarged layout at Durdham Downs giving kerbside loading for two routes. There were four tracks (two either side of a central island) to cope with the heavy traffic at Old Market Street (cars for Downs, Centre and Zetland Road not using the island, but pulling past it just round the corner where two could wait until the single line was clear); sidings for reversing cars at Bristol Bridge (this one was in use in horse tram days, and was moved to the pavement during the '20s), at Eastville, and at Zetland Road junction; and a covered tramway station on a spur at Temple Meads Joint Railway station, adapted from the former horse car depot. This station remained intact until 1945, when the G.W.R. staff canteen was opened on the site.

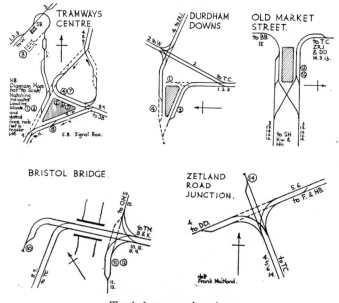

Track layout at junctions.
(Dotted tracks not often used.)

Many of the passing loops were protected by signals. The simplest of these consisted of a red disc with a white centre on one side and a white disc with a green ring on the other, which was operated by a man in a strategic position who could see both ends of the loop. Another type was a similar signal but electrically operated by a man at one end of the loop. Most of them, however, were operated by the passage of the trolley, the signal showing whether one or two cars were ahead occupying the loop. The most interesting signals were those installed in Perry Road where Downs—Centre and Downs—Old

Market routes diverged. The line from the Centre made a complete loop, altogether completing 250° and crossing the Old Market line at right angles before joining it. There were four semaphore signals worked from a small cabin built out from the side of the wall, from which the points were also controlled. This remained in use up to the passing of the last car, when it was dismantled. The place can still be seen as the new stonework has not weathered to the colour of the old.

The system abounded in steep gradients, of which the most severe was the 1 in 10 on Blackboy Hill. The sharpest curve had a radius of 30 feet. There were low railway bridges at Temple Meads, Stapleton Road station and Eastville; these carried a notice reading " Remain seated under Bridge. Do not touch overhead electric wires."

CURRENT COLLECTION.

Overhead trolley wire with swivel heads was used from the start, though the first cars had the trolley standard at one side (the south and east) of the cars and an unusual type of trolley head. By 1897 the trolley standard was moved to a position in the centre but offset longitudinally. Centre poles were used in Old Market Street (probably the first ever used in this country, and every other one carried

C. S. N. Walker.
Signals at Perry Road. Upper signal controls down cars, lower signal, cars from Horsefair. Signal box extreme right.

an arc light originally), by Lawrence Hill station, in Queen's Road, Whiteladies Road, up Blackboy Hill; in Baldwin Street and Victoria Street; in East Street and in Broadmead. Automatic trolley reversers were installed at practically every terminus between 1906 and 1910 and at several intermediate reversing places. Automatic point controllers and mechanical frogs were also in general use, though at Zetland Road Junction points and frogs were latterly operated by a switch on a standard. Most routes not having centre poles had span

*S. Miles Davey and C. S. N. Walker.*
No. 237, the highest numbered car, at Westbury terminus. Perry Road curve showing signals and signal box. Track to Tramways Centre on right, site of track to old horse depot in centre, track to Durdham Downs on left.

Double line of cars on the sidings at the back of Kingswood depot awaiting scrapping.

Brislington Depot. The left-hand pair of wires were erected in connection with trolleybus experiments.

wires, the wires being fixed by rosettes to the buildings in many cases, including an ornamental pair fixed to a church (now derelict) near The Mardyke, on the Hotwells route. There was little side arm construction except across The Downs on the Westbury route, where arms of exceptional length were employed. The wire used was at first of round section, but later grooved wire was universal.

Some experiments on trolley heads were carried out from a tower wagon especially equipped for the purpose.

### Depots.

These were seven in number, the largest being Brislington, which had running shed accommodation for 48 cars and also housed the repair shops. The others were at Horfield (capacity 55 cars), Staple Hill (38 cars), Eastville (28 cars), Bedminster (23 cars), Kingswood (22 cars), and St. George (19 cars). There was a small permanent way depot in Whitsun Street, St. Pauls, having a weighbridge on one track; although wired, this depot was only used by the rail grinders, and then very occasionally.

Kingswood Depot became the " graveyard " of the Bristol trams. In 1938, a hole was knocked out of the rear wall and a track laid through it out to the waste ground at the back of the premises, where double track sidings were put down. The entire fleet was broken up there, and in 1938/9 " funerals " were dealt with at the rate of a car a day. The method of destruction was that, first of all, the loose fittings were removed (many being sold to collectors), then the electrical equipment was dismantled, and finally the body was unbolted from the truck and, by means of block and tackle, pulled over sideways by the depot car. Being then upside down, the body was again hauled upright on the ground and set alight.

Of the other depots, Brislington, Eastville and Staple Hill were converted into bus garages, Horfield was sold to a private firm and St. George passed into the hands of the fire service.

### Generating Plant.

At the Counterslip Power House, the first unit to be installed (in 1900) was a 500 k.w. vertical cross compound steam set built by the Allis-Chalmers Company of America. Three additional sets of the same capacity followed shortly afterwards, and this plant handled the traction load plus the industrial requirements of the company—such as lighting in depots, offices and repair shops—until 1907. For the lighting of premises and track repair operations by night, however, the station also had two 100 k.w. and one 175 k.w. Bellis & Morcom engines and generators of the vertical compound

54

Three stages in breaking up the body: top, body
pulled off the frame; middle, being burnt; bottom,
the end.

centre valve type. The extra demand caused by the extensions of 1907/08 was met by the installation of a specially adapted vertical cross compound engine and generator of 1,000 k.w. capacity. The foregoing equipment sufficed for all purposes until 1928, when two 1,500 k.w. Adamson steam turbo sets were installed; these were geared by the Power Plant Co. to a five to one reduction and coupled to a Mather & Platt generator. The three small lighting sets were abandoned as redundant at the same time.

At the St. George Power House, the original plant of 1895 consisted of three sets of Willans patent centre valve compound type steam engines coupled to generators of 100 k.w. capacity each. This was later replaced by four Seymour compound tandem-coupled horizontal engines with generators of 150 k.w. capacity each. The engines were of the non-condensing type and were kept in readiness to assist the main plant at Counterslip in case of emergency. When not running in parallel with the main station, St. George handled the Kingswood and Hanham loads separately during peak hours.

# CLIFTON ROCKS RAILWAY

*B.T. & C. Co.. Ltd.*

View inside the Clifton Rocks Railway.  The conductor rode on the lower platform.

In addition to the street tramways, the company operated the Clifton Rocks Railway, a sub-surface version of the hydraulic counter-balance cliff tramways found at seaside resorts.  This line was built under the Gloucestershire side of the Avon Gorge and connected Hotwells with Clifton near the Bristol end of the Suspension Bridge. It was opened on 11th March, 1893, having taken two years to construct.* The tunnel, which was bored through solid rock on a gradient of 1 in 2.5, contained four tracks carrying two pairs of cars. The line at first carried very heavy traffic, but the closure in 1922 of the Port and Pier Railway, whose Hotwells station was situated near the lower terminus, robbed this railway of much of this traffic, and later the bus services from the Centre to Clifton also affected the receipts. For a long time through tickets were issued from Clifton to the Centre, available by Rocks Railway and the Hotwells tram route. The line was purchased by the Bristol Tramways & Carriage Co., Ltd. in November, 1912, and abandoned on 1st October, 1934. The tunnel was utilised during the recent war by the B.B.C. as emergency premises.

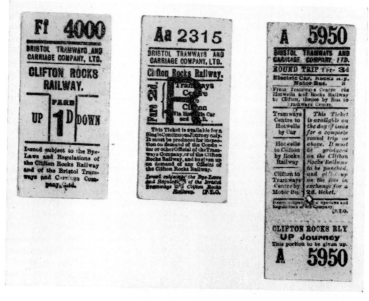

*Tickets courtesy B.T. & C. Co., Ltd.*

Early ticket issued on Rocks Railway (buff). Through ticket with Hotwells tram route (pink with red R). Note conditions about surrendering ticket. Round trip (pink). Note arrangements for auditing. There was a similar ticket for a journey in the reverse direction.

---

*A medallion was issued to passengers who travelled on the opening day.

# CAMBORNE

The only street tramway ever constructed in Cornwall was one which connected the tin-mining towns of Camborne and Redruth. The first effort to provide such a line was made in 1898, when application was made for a Light Railway Order in respect of a tramway 8.75 miles in length, between Camborne, Redruth and Portreath. This, however, was rejected owing to the narrowness of the roads and opposition by the Great Western Railway who objected on the grounds of physical interference.

The scheme was kept alive, however, and finally materialised in a modified form in 1900, when a Tramways Order was granted to the Urban Electric Supply Co., Ltd., for an electric tramway along the main road between Camborne and Redruth, a distance of three miles. Contracts for construction were placed with Messrs. Dick, Kerr and the B.T.-H. Co., Ltd., and the line was opened on 1st October, 1902, the inaugural car (No. 1) setting out from Camborne with members of the local board.

The tramway extended from the Commercial Square end of Trelowarren Street, Camborne, to the West End of Redruth, and was operated under the name of " Camborne & Redruth Tramways." The system was associated with the local electric lighting and power undertaking, and also with the Glossop Tramways in Derbyshire, which were also owned by the U.E.S. Co., Ltd.

In addition to the passenger service over the main route, the company carried tin ore under a contract with East Pool & Agar Ltd., between East Poole Mine and the Tolvaddon Stamps (i.e., Smelting Works). A private branch was laid in to serve each of these establishments, increasing the total route length of the tramways to 3.75 miles. Mineral traffic commenced in 1903.

Owing to motor bus competition and the general depression then reigning in this part of Cornwall, the company had to withdraw its passenger services on the 29th September, 1927, and the tramway undertaking was closed down shortly afterwards. Under the aegis of the electric light company, however, the section between the mines and the smelting works continued to carry mineral traffic, the necessary rolling stock and electrical equipment being maintained for this purpose. In 1934, however, the tramway became redundant owing

Nos. 2 and 3 passing.

*Courtesy C. Carter.*

*W. J. Bennetts & Sons.*

Inaugural car leaving Camborne.

to the installation of an aerial ropeway, and the remaining track and equipment were abandoned.

*Map: CAMBORNE & REDRUTH TRAMWAYS (Urban Electric Supply Co Ltd), showing Redruth, Camborne, and intermediate points. Labels include: Rly Stn, Post, West End, Plough Hotel, WEST END, Tolvear, G.W.R. to Truro, REDRUTH, Work-house, MAIN ROAD A30, Barncoose, ILLOGAN HIGHWAY, I.H. Hotel, LC, to Portreath, Mineral, Wheal Agar, East Pool Mine, POOL, Trevenson Gate, Industrial branch, CARN BREA, Mineral Branch, TALVADON STAMPS, Depot & Power Stn, LC East Hill, TUCKING MILL, Roskear, Dolcoath Road, MAIN ROAD A30, G.W.R. to Penzance, CAMBORNE, Centenary Chapel, TRELOWARREN STREET, Commercial Square, Stn. Scale: 1 M, 1 KM, 3/4, 1/2, 1/4, 0. JCG 252 after PWG.*

## SERVICES AND FARES.

Passenger cars maintained a 15 minute service from Monday to Thursday and a ten minute service on Friday and Saturday. The through ordinary fare was 4d. each way, and twopenny return tickets were available for workpeople.

## TICKETS.

The colour scheme was 1d. white, 2d. blue, 3d. green, 4d. red. There were also 3d., 5d. and 7d. returns, 1d. and 2d. child singles and 3d. and 4d. returns. The 1½d. child 1507 is yellow-green. All tickets were of a similar type.

## ROLLING STOCK.

Passenger traffic was operated with eight single-truck cars, all of which were unvestibuled and had Milnes trucks and B.T.-H. equipment including two 25 h.p. motors to each car. Six of them, namely those numbered 1-4, 7 and 8, were open-topped balcony cars with reversed stairs and three windows per side. Officially, these cars seated 50 passengers, but they regularly ran with over 100 up on football days and are reputed to have taken as many as 150 on occasions! Photographs of the first car show that it carried a peculiar kind of mesh lifeguard tray, but in later views, this has been replaced by the conventional wooden slat pattern and, in addition, slipper brakes have been fitted. The other two cars, Nos. 5 and 6, were single-deckers of the " combination " type, having a short centre saloon with two arched top windows on each side and an open-sided cross bench at each end.

For handling the mineral traffic, there were two four-wheeled

61

*W. J. Bennetts & Sons.*
No. 5 Milnes single-deck car at Commercial Square, Camborne.

*Photo E. V. Read, courtesy J. C. Gillham.*
Electric locomotive and ore train at East Poole Mine in 1926.

electric locomotives (one open and the other covered in), numbered 1 and 2 respectively and fitted with B.T.-H. equipment, and 12 ore wagons.

## LIVERY.

Dark green and cream with gold lining and "Camborne & Redruth" displayed on rocker panels.

## TRACK.

The main line was laid along the centre of the road with 83 lb. rails and was single throughout with nine passing loops. The tramway was of 3 ft. 6 in. gauge and was crossed on the level at three points by standard-gauge railways, the crossings occurring at Dolcoath Road, near East Hill, and at Illogan Highway respectively. The route was free from very severe gradients, the steepest being 1 in 15, and the sharpest curve was of 40 ft. radius. The two mineral branches were laid on private right of way and, as far as can be ascertained, were never used by passenger cars.

## CURRENT COLLECTION.

Overhead trolley fitted to one side of the car and bracket arm suspension. The poles, which were of a very plain design, are still in use for street lighting.

63

One of the two electric locomotives for handling mineral traffic.

## DEPOT.

This was built at Carnbrea, near the electricity works and at the junction of the spur to Tolvaddon Stamps. The premises are now used by the South Western Electricity Authority but have been considerably altered.

# CHELTENHAM

Unlike its neighbour, Gloucester, nine miles away, the spa town of Cheltenham had no tramways prior to the electric era and when they did come it was through enterprise from the U.S.A. In 1898, Mr. Thomas Nevins, an American pioneer of light railways in Gloucestershire, formed the Cheltenham & District Light Railway Co., Ltd., assisted by his son Mr. T. A. Nevins. Mr. Henry J. McCormick, a nephew, was appointed Construction Engineer and came over from the U.S.A. to take up his duties in 1901. Mr. Thomas Doyle was the Secretary to the company and under powers granted by Light Railway Orders in 1898 and 1899, work on the system commenced in 1901, Westinghouse being the contractors. He had previously (19th May, 1897) applied for powers to construct a line from the M.R. station to Winchcombe, nine miles of 3 ft. 6 in. gauge, to be worked by electricity " or other mechanical power," but this was rejected by the Light Railway Commissioners. A further application in June, 1899, for $5\frac{3}{4}$ miles from Lansdown Road to Cleeve Hill on a gauge of 4 ft. $8\frac{1}{2}$ in. was rejected, but later appeared in modified form.

The first route to be laid extended from Lansdown Castle (at the junction of Gloucester Road and Lansdown Road) to the summit of Cleeve Hill at a point just beyond the " Rising Sun," on which construction started from the Cleeve Hill end, 120 men being employed. There seems, however, to have been some delay in the delivery of materials, and a scarcity of skilled electricians, for the local Press says, *" These tramcars seem as uncertain a quantity up to now as a pro-Boer meeting! No doubt they exist somewhere in the precinct of one of the stations, and we have actually seen a picture† in the ' Chronicle & Graphic ' showing what they will look like when the postponements are postponed and the cars are running. But I have been patiently waiting, life insured and with fourpence in coppers ready for the last five weeks while all the fine weather has been placidly slipping away and never a car in sight."

However, the despondent writer had not much longer to wait, for on the 12th July, 1901, the first car ran on trial to the summit of Cleeve Hill. Later that month, 29th July, however, a disaster occurred

*' Gloucestershire Graphic,' 6th July, 1901.
†Of a Liverpool tram.

G

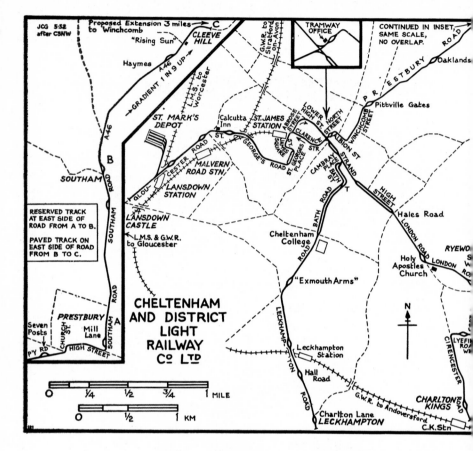

which caused a further setback, for a car ran away down the hill and overturned, causing the loss of two lives. It emerged in evidence that its slipper brakes had not been fitted as they were not ready.

The first official inspection of the line was made on Thursday, 15th August, 1901—" a beautiful summer's day following upon a series of wet ones "—by Col. Von Donop, R.E., of the Board of Trade, in the presence of Mr. Nevins and his son, Mr. Phillips, County Surveyor, Mr. J. Hall, the Cheltenham Surveyor, and Mr. McCormick, who acted as driver.

Confidence in the company's safety arrangements seems to have been shaken by the runaway, for we read *" I think the official party, numbering a baker's dozen, that took the trial trip on No. 5 car

---

*" Gleaner " in the ' Graphic,' 31st August, 1901.

deserve the warm thanks of the community for the confidence that they undoubtedly inspired among the public in the undertaking, whose reputation had been seriously shaken by the misadventure. I verily believe, from the observations I heard from bystanders and the anxious look on many of their faces, that they thought the party was going to certain destruction. The attendant procession of cycles and vehicles lent a suspicion to the assumption that the riders were determined to be in at the death. But all dismal forebodings were upset by the results achieved, and the wooden slipper brake, absent on the ill-fated car, now worked wonders on No. 5. And even the girls of Prestbury could scarce forbear a cheer as the car glided triumphantly back through the village. There was an anti-climax to the trip in the incident of an overturned wagon of straw on the track barring effectually the progress of No. 5. At all events we can now truly say:

> The August days were waning fast
> As through the streets of Chelt'nam passed
> Electric cars, all spruce and nice,
> Bearing aloft the same device—
> 'We ply for hire.'"

Public services commenced on 22nd August, car No. 7 being decorated with flags for the happy occasion, and on the first two

*From an early postcard.*
No. 2 in its original state with high lamp and
trolley standard at side, in High Street.

half days of operation, the trams carried 5,400 and 9,700 passengers respectively; by the end of the week the total had grown to 40,000. An amusing sidelight on the opening celebration is given in this Press report.* " These enterprising promoters did the thing well to their representative guests (as might be expected of them) at the formal opening christening of the line on 22nd August. And I think it ought to be mentioned, as further showing the kindly spirits of the hosts, they went out into the highways and byeways and called in the stragglers, including a ginger-beer vendor, to take a glass of the sparkling."

Traffic appears to have continued to improve, but by October, 1901, at a Town Council meeting, the tramway was called an eyesore, was of no public convenience, and it was said, " trams were of no utility in a town like Cheltenham." One member said he would vote strenuously against the extension of the tram lines to any other part of the Borough. Despite this and notwithstanding the admittedly numerous " teething troubles " which the company had to face, extensions were authorised in Light Railway Orders of 1903, the additional routes being those to Leckhampton and Charlton Kings. At the same time, a loop line was constructed from St. James' Square along Ambrose Street and High Street to the intersection at North Street corner, enabling cars to operate inwards by this route and outwards via Clarence Street. These sections were inspected by Major J. W. Pringle, R.E., on behalf of the Board of Trade on 28th March, 1905, and opened for public traffic on the same day, the then Mayor of Cheltenham driving one of the new batch of cars (No. 13) over the new routes during the opening ceremony. A note in the Press reads †" I hear that Mr. Nevins is well satisfied with the working up to the present. The Lower High Street section is now altogether abandoned, and I am not surprised to hear it, for the probable traffic on it would not have justified the expense of its laying."

The above note presumably refers to a proposed route from Calcutta Inn in the Gloucester Road, to the Gasworks and thence via Lower High Street to a junction at Ambrose Street.

The Leckhampton route terminated at the foot of the steep Leckhampton Hill, while the Charlton Kings terminus was just short of the G.W.R. Station. No further extensions were made after these, and the total route mileage of the system was 10.22.

In 1914, a new company was formed under the same title in association with Balfour, Beatty & Co., Ltd. (lessees of the Luton tramways and the controlling interest in numerous others), with Mr. McCormick as Director and General Manager, and thus reformed,

*" Gleaner " in the ' Graphic,' 31st August, 1901.
†" Gleaner " in the ' Graphic,' 22nd July, 1905.

the undertaking continued to operate until the growing popularity of the motor bus and the rapidly deteriorating condition of the tramway track and much of the rolling stock brought about its abandonment. Municipal opposition having disposed of a proposal to install trolley-buses, it was decided instead to replace the trams by motor buses, which took over the Cleeve Hill and Leckhampton routes in March, 1930. The last tram ran from Charlton Kings to the depot on 31st December the same year and the company at the same time changed its title to Cheltenham District Traction Co., Ltd. In that guise it continued to exist, later becoming a member of the " Red and White " group of bus companies, and is now, since nationalisation, under the control of the Bristol Omnibus Co.*

### SERVICES AND FARES.

The services were not numbered and were operated as follows:
Lansdown Castle—Cleeve Hill, with relief car Southam to Summit.

Frequency 30 mins. Time for double journey 1 hr. 45 mins.
Centre—Leckhampton, frequency 12 mins.

Time for double journey, 36 mins.
Lansdown Castle—Charlton Kings. Frequency 15 mins.

Time for double journey 75 mins.
Lansdown Castle—Southam. Frequency 15 mins.

Time for double journey 75 mins.

For about the last five years the Leckhampton cars were extended to St. James's Station to relieve the congestion caused by reversing at the centre, the company charging an extra penny for this short ride.

From about 1926 the Cleeve Hill and Southam cars reversed at North Street, so leaving only a 15 minute service, provided by the Charlton Kings cars to and from Lansdown and the Midland Station.

The single-deck cars of which further mention will be made later, had a curious use. Consequent on the runaway before the opening, the Board of Trade prohibited the carrying of passengers on the upper decks of cars on the hill section beyond Southam, and a single-decker was therefore kept in readiness there to take any passengers who had descended from the upper deck and who could not find seats in the saloon. For a short period, only the single-decker would climb the hill, and the two cars could be seen on the loop at the foot of the incline apparently indulging in " wrong line working." Also at one time both single-deckers were in use and during the winter they worked the through service to and from North Street with double-

*Since the 31st May, 1957, Bristol Omnibus Co., Ltd., though still operating in red livery.

deckers providing extra workings between Lansdown and Prestbury and Southam.

During the earlier years the days on which the Cheltenham Races were held saw the single-deckers transferred to the Leckhampton route to release additional double-deckers for transporting racegoers to and from the nearest point to the Prestbury racecourse.

A town office was opened in North Street and served as a waiting-room for Cleeve Hill passengers. From here a considerable parcel and luggage traffic was operated (later by two motor vans) and on the Cleeve Hill section morning papers, laundry and groceries were all delivered. Many times in winter the trams were the only vehicles to get through, a squad of stalwarts with shovels travelling out on the first car to clear a passage for it!

On Saturdays, Sundays and Bank Holidays the service was increased to every 7½ minutes to Southam, and every 15 minutes through to Cleeve Hill; the single-decker then worked a shuttle service up and down the hill completing three round trips in the hour.*

## TICKETS.

The fare stages were very irregular, 1d., 1½d., and 2d. stages giving rise to several sections over which the fare might be say 5½d. As in fact there was little demand for this ticket, many were used up by being surcharged by hand to another value. The fare to Cleeve Hill from North Street varied from 6d. to 9d. single and various reductions were offered to bulk buyers. On the single-decker tickets were cancelled by a further club-shaped cancellation as can be seen on one of the tickets reproduced.

The colour scheme varied somewhat with fare changes, but by the early '20s the following colours were established. 1d. white, 1½d. salmon, 2d. orange, 2½d. blue, 3d. pink, 3½d. purple, 4d. green, 4½d. grey, 5d. buff, 5½d. lilac, 6d. white and later apple green, 7d. grey, 7½d. primrose, 8d. purple, 9d. orange and later yellow, 10½d. olive green and 1/- pale blue. Later issues had the fare overprinted. Return tickets were mostly white with coloured edges. Child or workman single 1d. were white—special sections of ordinary tickets were used for higher values of half fares. On the Cleeve Hill section a club-shaped cancellation was used when the passenger travelled on the single-deck car. Examples illustrated are 2d. buff 5159, as in use prior to 1920. 6d. apple green 5530 the type in use from mid-'20s onwards; this example shows the club-shaped cancellation. 1/- return, white with red stripe, 7540 was used on the Cleeve Hill route

*On Saturday afternoons and Bank Holidays the Leckhampton service also was increased to every 7½ minutes.

the date being indicated by the punch hole. With fare revisions several values became obsolete and many were used up by being surcharged; 2d. on 5½d. lilac 6633 is such an example.

ROLLING STOCK.

The first batch of cars (Nos. 1-8) were built in the U.S.A. by the J. Stephenson Car Company. They were imported at Avonmouth Docks, Bristol, and forwarded to Cheltenham by G.W.R. These cars were open-top double-deckers having four drop windows each side, reversed stairs, red plush upholstered longitudinal seating inside and the headlamp fitted on the canopy. The dashboards on them curved round more fully towards the step than usual, thus giving the cars the appearance of being broader than they actually were. They were mounted on Peckham single trucks and provided with electro-magnetic and mechanical track brakes, which latter were applied by a separate wheel on the nearside of the controller. This and the ordinary handbrake column were fitted outside the dash. The cars seated 48 (26/22).

The remark of a local councillor, quoted earlier on, about the trams being " an eyesore and of no convenience to the public " was perhaps to some extent justified, for when first put into service, these cars carried nothing but wire mesh and guard rails around the upper deck and had no indicators whatever! These deficiencies, however, were made good 'ere long, for the conventional panelling was put on and roller indicator boxes were fitted on the top guard rails in 1905. In about 1915, however, these indicators were removed and all the cars were fitted with reversible indicator boards on the outside bottom of the centre windows; about a year later these were supplemented by reversible boards hung from the canopies. These remained in use until 1923 when the original roller boxes were again brought into use on all cars except the single-deckers. Shortly afterwards the side boards were removed from the outside of the windows and placed inside.

Next came two single-deckers (Nos. 9 and 10) which were built in 1902 for the Cleeve Hill route by the Gloucester Railway Carriage & Wagon Co., Ltd. They were, in effect, the bottom half of the double-deckers less the stairs, being indentical in every respect. They had seats for three on each platform. Shortly afterwards came Nos. 11 and 12, which were further open-toppers of the 1-8 type but built by the Gloucester firm.

These 12 cars were subjected to a good deal of alteration in their time. First of all No. 1 was rebuilt in 1916 and had its head-lamps lowered to dashboard level. No. 11 was rebuilt in 1917 and was the first to appear in the wartime grey livery. About 1923 No. 9 was rebuilt and converted into a double-decker, taking all the top deck fittings from No. 12 which then became a single-decker; these two cars remained thus until the end. No. 2 was temporarily

*Gloucester R.C. & W. Co., Ltd.*
One of the original single-deck cars built for the Cleeve Hill route.

converted into a single-decker while No. 9 was being rebuilt, but upon No. 12 being put into service as a single-decker No. 2 was again made a double-decker. Another car—No. 3—latterly had its top deck removed but as No. 10 had by then been scrapped it will be seen that at no time were there more than two single-deckers—in the early days Nos. 9 and 10, and later Nos. 3 and 12.

The following cars of the 1-12 group had their original trucks replaced by the Brill 21E type—Nos. 1, 2, 3, 4, 7, 8 and 9; some of the red plush seat covering gave place to cane straw, and in later

*Photo courtesy Bristol Omnibus Co. Ltd.*
No. 7 at Southam with early type destination box.

73

No. 20 at Leckhampton. *From a postcard.*

*From a postcard.*
No. 10 at Cleeve Hill. Note trolley standard at side.

years Nos. 1, 2, 5, 6, 7 and 8 had their slipper brakes removed and consequently did not again operate on the Cleeve Hill section; they were mainly used on the Lansdown-Charlton Kings route and very occasionally were seen at Leckhampton.

In 1905, eight new cars were acquired for the Leckhampton and Charlton Kings extensions. These, numbered 13-20, were more normal looking three window open-toppers with reversed stairs, longitudinal cane straw seating in the saloon, Peckham trucks, Westinghouse equipment and headlamps on the dash. They were not, however, fitted with slipper brakes and therefore were not allowed up Cleeve Hill. No. 18 was rebuilt about 1922 and was later fitted with a Brill 21E truck though this was afterwards changed again to an original Peckham type. Nos. 14 and 15 were also later given Brill 21E trucks. The first major alteration in these cars occurred in 1927 when No. 14 was completely rebuilt and modernised: it was vestibuled and had panelled dashboards, the stairs being changed to the normal position; the number was altered to 10, the single-decker with this number having then been scrapped; the longitudinal seats were covered in brown leather and the car mounted on a new Peckham Pendulum truck which gave very comfortable riding.

*From a postcard.*
No. 1 and single-deck car at Southam.

75

The following year No. 16 appeared similarly rebuilt with the same improvements as the new No. 10 and with a somewhat unusual all-white interior decoration which caused it to be nicknamed " The Bathroom." The longitudinal seats were covered with grey and white plush; this car retained its original number. Shortly afterwards another of this class, No. 19, was similarly modernised and was renumbered 1, the original No. 1 being by this time worn out and taken out of service. This new No. 1 was the last car to receive any major attention, no further repainting and renovating being undertaken. These three cars—Nos. 1, 10, and 16—with their rebuilt bodies and new trucks provided excellent service on the Lansdown-Charlton Kings and Leckhampton routes until the closing of the system and it is to be regretted that their new lease of life was so short.

No further additions were made until after the war, when, in 1921, the company took delivery of three new English Electric cars of a much improved design. These were Nos. 21-23 and were actually part of an order for four, the remaining car being diverted to the associated system at Leamington. They were four window vestibuled

*The late Dr. H. A. Whitcombe.*
No. 10, originally No. 14 but rebuilt with normal stairs, vestibuled and mounted on a new truck.

open-toppers of neat appearance having normal stairs, transverse wooden seats on both decks, and Peckham Pendulum trucks with 7 ft. wheelbase. Their equipment was by Metro-Vick and included electro-magnetic track brakes combined with Westinghouse controllers. These units were kept almost exclusively on the Prestbury and Cleeve Hill section, largely superseding the single-deckers.

Finally, in 1928, the company brought two cars from the Worcester tramways whose Nos. 16 and 17 became Nos. 25 and 24 respectively at Cheltenham. These cars, which were semi-vestibuled and mounted on Brill 21E trucks, had longitudinal polished wooden seating in the lower saloon. They were used almost entirely on the Leckhampton route, No. 24 being the last car to run on the final night of operation on this section.

Cars Nos. 21-25 never carried side indicator boards as the use of these had by then been discontinued, as also was the case with the latterly rebuilt cars Nos. 1, 10 and 16. Differing from the final position on all the other cars Nos. 24 and 25 had the roller boxes placed above the top guard rail.

The only service vehicle was a four-wheeled ballast truck for use on the reserved track, and this when required was hitched to a passenger car and parked on one of the disused loops. On one occasion it was being run down the hill light and ran away owing to its brakes not being designed for such continuous application. It derailed on the curve near the bottom and the man who was riding on it was killed. Double-decker No. 8 was periodically fitted up for rail grinding duties, also single-decker No. 9 prior to its being rebuilt.

The body of No. 22 until recently stood in a field near the main Gloucester road at Staverton, while that of No. 21 or 23 may still be found on a farm in Kingsditch Lane, between the Tewkesbury road and Swindon Village. Nos. 9 and 10 became part of a gipsy encampment between Badgeworth and Churchdown. Ex-Worcester No. 25 did duty as a caddies' hut on Lilley Brook Golf Course, while the saloon part of double-decker No. 13 is still in use as a bus shelter at the Cleeve Hill terminus.

Cars 1, 9, 10, 16 and 21-23 were retained for some time after the system closed with a view to their being transferred to the Llandudno and Colwyn Bay line, but this did not take place.

### LIVERY.

Originally the cars were finished in plain dark red but later medium lake and cream was adopted as the standard colour scheme. During the war, shortage of paint reduced the fleet to a sorry state and in 1917-18 cars 6, 11, 12, 13, 16 and 20 were given a coat of battleship grey to preserve them. The full colours, however, returned

*'Cheltenham Chronicle.'*
English Electric car, as delivered in 1921, entering St. Mark's depot.

and special attention was given to the interior of No. 9, the ceiling
being panelled in grey and artistically lined out. The car numbers
were always displayed at each end of the waist panel as well as on
the dash, and the rocker panels were inscribed " CHELTENHAM &
DISTRICT LIGHT RAILWAY."

## TRACK.

The system was of 3 ft. 6 in. gauge and the total length of track
was 12.23 miles. The original line from Lansdown to Cleeve Hill
was single-and-loop throughout, laid with 80 lb. rails, and had
staggered rail joints. Beyond Oaklands, where it left the town and
entered the country, the track occupied the extreme south side of the
road and after passing the village of Prestbury, ran on its own right
of way along the east side of the road; so close to the side was it in
fact, that the car windows were often brushed by the hedge! The
reserved track was laid very lightly on sleepers with insufficient ballast
and gave very rough riding, motormen having to exercise great care
over points and some rail joints. The long climb from Southam to
the summit included the steepest gradient on the system, 1 in 8.9.

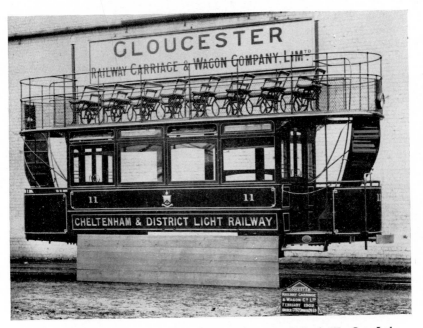

*Gloucester R.C. & W. Co., Ltd.*
Body for one of the original type cars as built without upper deck decency
boards.

The 1905 extensions were constructed with heavier rails weighing
90 lb. per yard and included double track in High Street and Bath
Road. Except for some curves (with which the system abounded, the
sharpest being 37 ft. radius) and most of the points, no relaying
was done and in later years the track deteriorated rapidly to an almost
unsafe condition. A trailing crossover at the town end of Bath Road
was apparently never used.

### CURRENT COLLECTION.

Current collection was by overhead wire with swivel trolley heads.
On the original routes, side brackets on the east side of the road
were used almost exclusively, and except for a small portion in
London Road and Leckhampton Road where span wires were used, the
rest of the system was also equipped with side arms, though not
necessarily always on the same side of the road. Various, and often
unsuccessful, experiments in wire suspension were carried out in the
early days, but latterly the standard 8 section wire was used and gave
no trouble. Trolleys were turned by a rope kept wound round the
trolley-pole on double-deckers, and hooked up on the standard on

single-deckers. At the North Street and Cambray junctions frogs were of the pull-off type. There were no signals of any sort over the single line sections.*

The trolley standards on cars 1-12 were originally mounted to one side of the car (in practice, the east side) but were moved to the centre about 1912. Many of the poles are still in use for street lighting.

## DEPOT.

These premises were erected alongside the then Midland Railway cutting to the north of Lansdown Station and designated St. Mark's Depot. There were three tracks under cover, giving stabling for 25 cars and one track outside. Repairs, rebuilding and painting were carried out there. The depot now forms part of the company's bus garage and the track in the private road leading to it is still in place, covered in tarmac.

---

*In the application of 1899 the County Council wanted signals through Prestbury.

# EXETER

## HORSE TRAMWAYS.

The history of the tramways in this city commences in the year 1880, when the Exeter Tramways Company, Ltd. was formed by three promoters named Moore, Bidder and Buckland. The first route was opened on 6th April, 1882, between the Bude Hotel at the corner of High Street and Paris Street and the Diocesan Training College in Heavitree Road. It was operated with two single-deck cars which, according to local records, were " approximately 14 ft. long, 10 ft. high and 5 ft. wide with seating for 12 passengers with another four at the rear (outside); they were painted yellow and chocolate with the company's monogram on a yellow ground. The roof was extended to give protection to the outside passengers." Between 800 and 900 passengers were carried on Good Friday, 1882, and on 23rd May

*Photo courtesy Exeter City Transport Dept.*
Horse tram at Queens' Junction. Note overhead already erected in High St. From the accompanying photograph it would appear that there were also double-deck cars.

the same year an extension along Heavitree Road to Livery Dole (Midway Terrace) was brought into use.

By the end of the year, the company had opened a second route. This extended from the Obelisk at the junction of the New North Road and Queen Street to Blackboy Road (Idol Lane), and although the company wanted to run their cars along Queen Street and High Street, stiff opposition by traders in those important thoroughfares, who feared that the presence of trams there would injure their custom, caused the company to use the less-frequented route along New North Road. Such prejudice was typical of the times, but, nevertheless, on 1st August, 1883, this route was extended at both ends—westwards to St. David's Station (G.W.R.) and eastwards along Pinhoe Road to Polsloe Road. These were, however, the last sections to be constructed by the company and, in fact, the St. David's Station route, which was poorly patronised, was subsequently reduced to a service on Market Days only and later still ceased operation altogether. Indeed, the company's affairs generally seemed to have gone badly very soon for as early as April, 1883, there was a Petition in Chancery for its winding up, and at one period the tramways, together with a few local horse-buses, were run by a concern called the " Tramways Purchase Syndicate." Then, in 1903, the undertaking was acquired by the Exeter Corporation and electrified, with the exception of the track along New North Road and the depot there, which were abandoned. During their last year of operation, the horse trams

*The late G. N. Southerden.*
No. 22 in original condition on
Pinhoe Road route, 1926.

carried over 400,000 passengers, the route mileage at that time being 2 miles 30 chains.

<h2 style="text-align:center">ELECTRIC TRAMWAYS.</h2>

The original opposition having now subsided, tracks were laid in High Street and Queen Street, and on 4th April, 1905, the first electric cars entered service between the Guildhall and Heavitree Road (Midway Terrace) and between St. David's Station and Pinhoe

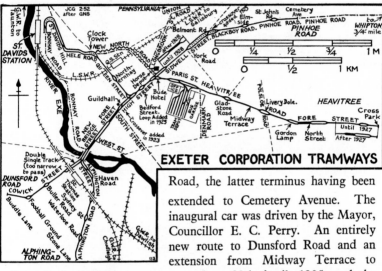

**EXETER CORPORATION TRAMWAYS**

Road, the latter terminus having been extended to Cemetery Avenue. The inaugural car was driven by the Mayor, Councillor E. C. Perry. An entirely new route to Dunsford Road and an extension from Midway Terrace to Cross Park, Heavitree, were opened on 29th April, 1905, and the system was completed by the opening of the Alphington Road line on 22nd September, 1906. The routes were all quite short and totalled only 4.95 miles. Several other proposed routes totalling about three miles were not proceeded with and a scheme to electrify the abandoned New North Road track was also dropped.

Despite several improvements made during the 'twenties and even a proposed extension of the Pinhoe Road route to Whipton, for which powers were actually obtained in 1928, the system began to decline about this time in favour of motor buses, and in July, 1930, the greater part of the Alphington Road line was abandoned. The other routes were all withdrawn during 1931, all sections west of the Guildhall being closed on 6th July and Pinhoe Road on 5th August. On the latter date also, the Heavitree route was curtailed at Paris Street Depot, and was worked as a shuttle service until 19th August, 1931, when the last Exeter tram No. 14, one of the older open-toppers bedecked with flags, etc., was driven to the depot by Mr. Perry, who had been at the "throttle" of the first car.

## SERVICES.

As previously stated, the inaugural services were Guildhall-Heavitree and St. David's-Pinhoe Road. With the opening of the Dunsford Road and Heavitree extensions, these two routes were paired up as a cross-city service, and when the Alphington Road line was brought into use in 1906, the Pinhoe Road cars were diverted to serve it in a similar fashion. The St. David's Station section was thereafter worked as a shuttle service to and from the foot of Queen Street.

A system of coloured signs was introduced to indicate the various services, these being displayed at each end of the upper deck and in the centre side window. Pinhoe Road-Alphington Road had a green disc on a white background; Dunsford Road-Heavitree, a white cross on a red background; and Queen Street-St. David's, a white disc on a green background.

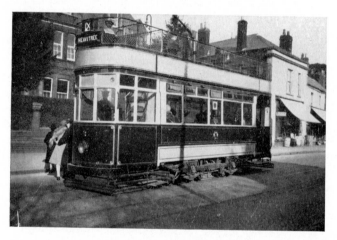

*The late G. N. Southerden.*
No. 2 of the 1929 1-4 batch. Note odd window layout. At Midway Terrace, 1929.

## TICKETS.

The early colour scheme with full geographical tickets was ½d. salmon (9049), 1d. blue, 1½d. green, with the fare overprinted. In later years, stages only were printed, and the colour scheme changed to 1d. white (5591), 1½d. salmon or blue, 2d. buff, 2½ green, 3d. grey. Return tickets were the same but overprinted R (3d. 7984 and 1½d. 1660) and sometimes a band of colour (1d. Return 1981 has a purple stripe on white). The Tramways Purchase Syndicate operated

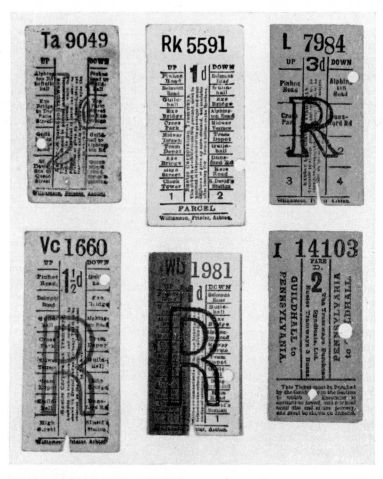

the system for a short while before the Corporation took over. The 2d. light blue, is unusual in having a five-figure serial number. The large punch hole indicates that it was cancelled by an early type of bell punch.

## ROLLING STOCK.

The first batch of cars was delivered in 1905 by Dick, Kerr & Co., and consisted of 14 four-wheelers having three side windows, end balconies, normal stairs and seating for 42 persons. They had D.K. 25 h.p. motors, Westinghouse equipment (including magnetic brakes) and Brill 21E trucks, and were numbered 1-12, 14 and 15. Cars 16-21, of the same type, followed in 1906 and were distinguishable from the earlier ones by their higher guard rails around the upper deck.

Further additions to the fleet were also of the open-top four-wheel pattern with three-window bodywork but were supplied by Brush. Nos. 22-25 came in 1914 and had 34 h.p. motors and a seating capacity of 44, whilst Nos. 26 and 27, delivered in 1921, were larger cars with 54-seat bodies mounted on Peckham P.22 long-wheelbase trucks; the latter cars originally had mechanical track brakes and were mostly confined to the Pinhoe Road route. Nos. 28-34 were the first vestibuled trams in Exeter and were fitted with electric bells; they had 7 ft. wheelbase, Brill 21E trucks, 40 h.p. motors, and seating for 54 (30 outside and 24 inside). The first three (28-30) were built in 1925 and the other four in 1926.

From 1926 onwards, cars 19, 22, 23, 24, 26 and 27 were rebuilt with vestibules and angular dashboards, the first four also being fitted with Ackley's patent vertical hand-brake wheel in place of the familiar handle. In the absence of any car numbered 13—presumably on grounds of superstition!—and owing to the withdrawal of No. 12 as a result of damage sustained on 7th March, 1917, when she ran away down Fore Street and turned over on Exe Bridge, there were never more than 32 cars in stock at any one time. Parts from the ill-fated No. 12 were used for much-needed repairs to the rest of the fleet, which, in common with those of many other systems,

*The late G. N. Southerden.*
No. 19 (later 21) at St. David's Station, 1926.

suffered considerably through lack of maintenance during the war years.

In 1929, four of the early cars, namely Nos. 1, 5, 7 and 17, were replaced by four new vestibuled cars of generally similar design to the 28-34 series and also of Brush manufacture. These seated 53 passengers and the interior appointments were of a much improved standard, with upholstered transverse seats arranged on the " 2 and 1 " plan. The bodies had five side windows, of which three on each side were smaller than the other two, and were mounted on P35 trucks. These cars, which were the last trams to be built for any West Country system, took the numbers 1-4, and to accommodate them, the following renumbering took place in conjunction with the withdrawal of the four older vehicles:

> Original No.  2 became No.  5.
> Original No.  3 became No.  7.
> Original No.  4 became No. 19.
> Original No. 19 became No. 21.
> Original No. 17 withdrawn.

Nos. 2, 3 and 4, after renumbering carried their old numbers in black below the used ticket box. The renumbering of 19 to 21 was said to have been aimed chiefly at bringing all the vestibuled cars into one continuous series, but as it happened, No. 25 was not rebuilt so the series remained incomplete. The new No. 19 (ex-4) became something of an anomaly being a car with low guard rails brought into a class with high ones.

Cars numbered up to 25 originally had their destination indicators fitted on standards above the guard rails, but these were soon moved to a position under the canopy. They had no box for the route sign, which consisted merely of a metal disc, and had the top-deck lamps mounted on the end of the guard rails. On those cars which were rebuilt, however, the indicators were again moved to the top deck above the end sheeting and surmounted by a small box for the sign, and the lamps were transferred to the head of the stairs, these alterations all being in conformity with standard features of cars acquired after 1914. Magnetic track brakes were fitted throughout the fleet.

On the abandonment of the system, cars 1-4 being barely two years old, were sold to the Halifax Corporation Tramways, while Nos. 26, 27 and 28-34 went to Plymouth Corporation.

One of the chief reasons why none of the Exeter trams ever had top covers was the existence of two low railway bridges across the Dunsford Road and Alphington Road routes; the former, at St Thomas Station, still carries a notice warning passengers to " keep their seats, please!"

*L. Storry.*

No. 19 as rebuilt; at St. David's Station.

## LIVERY.

Until 1925, the cars were finished in dark green lined in gold for the waist, dash, stairs and cant rail, and cream lined in brown for the rocker and upper panelling, with the numerals and title in gold shaded with pink. A smart touch was added by painting the truck sides green (some were even lined in yellow) instead of the customary black, and lifeguard gear was maroon.

In March, 1925, a new and rather more attractive shade of light green—officially known as "napier green"—was introduced on car No. 23 and later became standard. The gold lining became more elaborate in the new livery and from 1928 onwards the thick and thin gold lines were replaced by thick gold and thin white lines, although this style did not have time to become standard.

According to the late G. N. Southerden, Exeter trams were originally very dark green, lined gold and ivory lined brown. Trucks were green lined yellow, trolley masts and destination boxes black. Title in gold shaded red.

In the late 1920s a brighter shade of green was adopted, including the trolley mast. The gold lettering was omitted.

## TRACK.

The total mileage of track under operation was 7.78, the majority of which was single; there was, however, double track on the outer portion of the St. David's route and in Blackboy Road, while between Exe Bridge and St. Thomas Station there was a curious section of double line of which the two tracks were laid so close together that two cars could not pass one another. The only possible advantage in such "double single" track must have been the saving in points! The gauge of the system was 3 ft. 6 in. and the rails used weighed 90 lb. per yard. There was no reserved track, but automatic signals were installed on three of the single line sections, namely, Paris Street, Heavitree Road (Polsloe Road to Gordon Lamp) and Cowick Street (Exe Bridge junction to Buller Road). The Bude Hotel and Exe Bridge junctions were provided with automatic point controllers. The steepest gradient was the 1 in 11.5 on which car No. 12 disgraced herself, while the sharpest curve had a radius of 30 feet.

### CURRENT COLLECTION.

The orthodox overhead trolley system with swivel heads was used, most of the construction being of the side bracket type, although there were centre poles in Blackboy Road and on St. David's Hill. Round section 4-0 wire with soldered ears was used. The last of the poles are now being removed after having served as lighting standards since the trams ceased operation. One of the breaker boxes at Exe Bridge is still in existence for traffic light control and has lately been repainted. There were no automatic trolley reversers.

### DEPOT.

This was located on the south side of Paris Street and had five roads and a short bay. Four tracks were provided with pit facilities. The premises are now used as the Corporation's bus garage.

# GLOUCESTER

## HORSE TRAMWAYS.

Tramways for the City of Gloucester were first proposed in 1877, when The Gloucester Tramways Co., Ltd., submitted details of a projected system to the City Council. Mr. (later Sir) George White, one of the pioneers of the Bristol Tramways, was also one of the promoters of the Gloucester scheme, the new company being a subsidiary of The Imperial Tramways Co., Ltd. Municipal sanction was finally given in the following January, and the company obtained an order under the Tramways Act for the construction of the lines in April, 1878, the authorised route length being 3 miles 51 chains. Construction was put in hand in September of the same year, and after approval had been given by Col. Hutchinson of the Board of Trade, services were inaugurated on 24th May, 1879—apparently all on the same day and without the formal opening ceremony usually connected with such events.

Permission to operate steam engines had been applied for, but, though this was approved by the Commons, the House of Lords rejected it.

The system as then opened comprised four routes, radiating, one in each direction, from the Cross, the city's central point and sometimes described as the Cross Roads of England, with a branch along Worcester Street to Kingsholm. Services were operated as follows:

> Wotton (Fleece Inn) - London Road - Northgate Street - Cross - Southgate Street - Theresa Place (Bristol Road).
>
> Kingsholm (Denmark Road) - Northgate Street - Cross - The Royal Infirmary (Southgate Street).
>
> India Road - Lower Barton Street - Eastgate Street - Cross - St. Nicholas Church.

and later:

> Cross - Eastgate Street - Clarence Street - Railway Stations.*

Owing to the fact that the Westgate Street section was not laid to the full extent of its authorised length, i.e. to St. Bartholomew Hospital, the route length of the system as constructed was 3 miles 32 chains, and the total cost of construction and equipment was £30,593. The

---

*The Midland Station in those days was on the site of the present cattle sidings.

cars, of which there were six at the opening, were built by the Bristol Wagon Co., and the Loughborough Locomotive and Engineering Works and were allocated four to the Fleece Inn-Theresa Place route, and one each to the India House - St. Nicholas Church, and Kingsholm - Infirmary routes. These and subsequent cars which were obtained also from the Gloucester Railway Carriage & Wagon Co., Ltd., including one " of a special type for carrying luggage " for the stations route, were all single-deckers, as the 4 ft. gauge to which the lines were constructed was considered too narrow for knife-board roof seats. A 15 minute service was maintained on the main route, and a 20 minute service on the other two routes. The original fare was a universal twopence rate, but this was soon reduced to 1d. No tickets were issued. The fleet was subsequently expanded to 13 cars and comprised two types—saloon cars seating 22 and " summer cars " seating 24 passengers on four cross benches, protected, when necessary, by side curtains. A stud of 45 horses was maintained and the depot and stables were at India Road. The car crews worked a 77 hour week when the fare was 1d. from the Cross anywhere.

In his 'Tramways, their Construction and Working,' Volume 2, 1881, D. K. Clark gives the following statistics in respect of the working of the tramways for the year ended 30th June, 1880:

| | | |
|---|---|---|
| Gross receipts ... | ... | £3,156. |
| Working expenses | ... | £3,930. |
| Deficit ... ... | ... | £774. |
| Passengers carried | ... | 716,226. |
| Car miles run ... | ... | 135,857. |

The tramways were initially popular largely on account of the novelty of " vehicles gliding rapidly and frequently through the streets of Gloucester, and knots of ' corner men ' gazed at them with much of the wonder the heathen Chinese bestowed on the first steam engine which entered the Celestial Empire,"* but the concern soon got into difficulties, and in July, 1881, was sold to a new company, the City of Gloucester Tramways Co., Ltd., with Mr. George White as secretary, for the sum of £8,000.† The line to the Railway Stations via Clarence Street and the Westgate Street section, which had become a liability owing to the paucity of traffic, were both abandoned, and thereafter passengers for the Great Western Station were catered for by the Wotton cars, and passengers for the (new) Midland Station by the India Road cars. A short length of track in Westgate Street at the Cross was left in position for reversing India Road cars. The undertaking then carried on more profitably and in 1895 an Order was obtained authorising extensions from Theresa Place along Bristol

*'Gloucester Journal,' 31st May, 1879.
†Some accounts record £18,000.

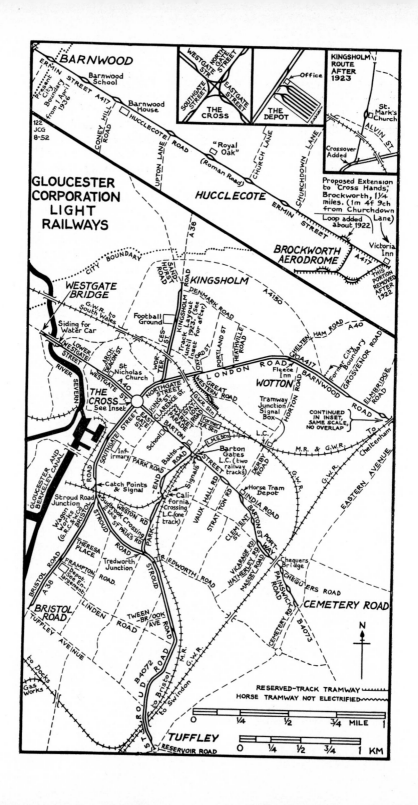

GLOUCESTER
CORPORATION
LIGHT
RAILWAYS

BARNWOOD

THE CROSS

THE DEPOT

KINGSHOLM ROUTE AFTER 1923

Proposed Extension to "Cross Hands", Brockworth, 1¼ miles. (1m 4f 9ch from Churchdown Lane)

Loop added about 1922

THIS PORTION REMOVED AFTER 1922

BROCKWORTH AERODROME

HUCCLECOTE

"Royal Oak"
(Roman Road)

Barnwood School
Barnwood House

WESTGATE BRIDGE

KINGSHOLM

WOTTON

THE CROSS
See Inset

RESERVED-TRACK TRAMWAY
HORSE TRAMWAY NOT ELECTRIFIED

BRISTOL ROAD

CEMETERY ROAD

TUFFLEY

N

0   ¼   ½   ¾  MILE  1

0   ¼   ½   ¾   1 KM

122
JCG
8-52

Road to Tuffley Avenue, and along the Painswick Road to Cemetery Road, and also to convert the whole system to electric operation. The Bristol Road extension was duly opened (for horse cars) on 10th July, 1897, but the other extension was not proceeded with, and horse traction continued. There were now 14 cars and 100 horses and an additional depot at Bristol Road.

In November, 1899, the company, without any previous arrangement with the Corporation, made an application to the Light Railway Commissioners for an Order authorising them to construct and work Light Railways in and near the City of Gloucester, in place of the existing Horse Tramways, with certain extensions, and on a gauge of 3 ft. 6 in. The routes to be electrified are described as:

No. 1. 4 miles 2 furlongs 3 chains. Commencing in Bristol Road opposite Tuffley Avenue, and passing along Bristol Road, Southgate Street, The Cross, Northgate Street, London Road, Ermine Street and Barnwood Road to a point near the Churchdown Lane at Hucclecote.

*Gloucester R.C. & W. Co., Ltd.*
Summer type of horse tram in the maker's yard.

93

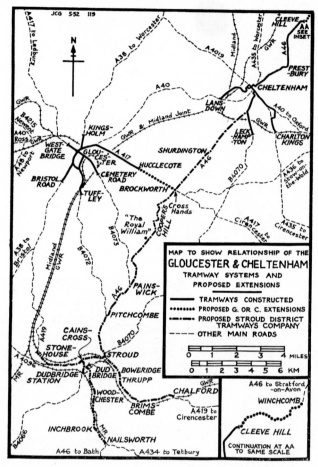

MAP TO SHOW RELATIONSHIP OF THE
**GLOUCESTER & CHELTENHAM**
TRAMWAY SYSTEMS AND
PROPOSED EXTENSIONS

| | |
|---|---|
| ━━━━━ | TRAMWAYS CONSTRUCTED |
| •••••••• | PROPOSED G. OR C. EXTENSIONS |
| ━·━·━·━ | PROPOSED STROUD DISTRICT TRAMWAYS COMPANY |
| ─────── | OTHER MAIN ROADS |

No. 1a.  1.15 chains.  Commencing in Southgate Street and curving into Eastgate Street so as to connect Nos. 1 and 2.

No. 2.  1 mile 7 furlongs 1.51 chains.  Commencing at Westgate Bridge and passing along Westgate Street, The Cross, Eastgate Street, Barton Street, Lower Barton Street, and Portway as far as Cemetery Road.

No. 3.  1 mile 2 furlongs 1.90 chains.  Commencing in Stroud Road, opposite Tuffley Avenue, and passing along Stroud Road to join No. 1 in the Bristol Road.

No. 4.  4 furlongs 2.53 chains.  Commencing by a junction with No. 1 in Northgate Street and passing along Worcester Street and Kingsholm Road to a point near the Sandhurst Road.

Total length of route: 7 miles 7 furlongs 8.94 chains.

The report of the Tramways Committee to the Council dated April, 1902, states " The existing Horse Tramways are discreditable to the Tramway Company and to the City, and the Omnibus traffic had proved an intolerable nuisance and caused much damage to the roads both within and beyond the City. As it has long been felt that the Horse Tramways and Omnibuses should give place to a thoroughly efficient and up-to-date system of Electric Tramways or Light Railways; and as the right of the Corporation to purchase the tramways would not accrue until 1911, the Corporation deemed it advisable to facilitate the earlier conversion of the Tramways into Electric Light Railways, and some negotiations took place between the Corporation and the Company but nothing had been arranged at the date of the Inquiry held by the Light Railway Commissioners. However, in the hope of avoiding delay, it was agreed that the Corporation should conditionally acquiesce in the application of the Company, and the County and City were both represented at the Inquiry and acquiesced in the application of the Company which was then unopposed. The Committee cannot therefore understand why the County Council should now object to the granting of an Order giving the Corporation similar powers to those which would have been granted to the Company . . . Unfortunately the Corporation were unable to arrange terms with the Company, who, in November, 1900, broke off the negotiations, which resulted in a year being wasted.

" A few months ago the Mayor reopened the negotiations and the Corporation have now provisionally agreed for the purchase of the Tramways undertakings, property and effects of the Company, including their interests in the proposed Light Railway Order; but the Corporation are obliged to take over the whole of the Omnibuses, Char-a-bancs, horses, etc. belonging to the Company, as well as the Tramways, and these will involve a considerable loss to the City, while the County will be indirectly benefited by their being eventually taken off the road on the construction of the proposed Corporation Light Railways."

The same report continues: " It is essential that any Light Railway along the Barnwood and Hucclecote Roads should belong to and be worked with and as part of the City system of Light Railways; and though the present application only provides for making a railway as far as Hucclecote, the Corporation would be prepared in due course to extend it to The Cross Hands, Brockworth, in order to facilitate an exchange of passengers to and from the proposed Light Railway from Painswick to Cheltenham." This refers to part of the Stroud District Tramways system. Promoted by Mr. Nevins of Cheltenham, it was proposed to run from Stroud to Chalford, near the station; to Nailsworth via Dudbridge with a branch to Dudbridge Station; to

Stonehouse railway bridge; to Painswick and Cheltenham. In spite of opposition it was passed by the Light Railway Commissioners with the exception of the Painswick - Cheltenham section, but work was never proceeded with.

"Some time ago the County Council intimated that they did not consider it advisable that another Local Authority should construct and own a Light Railway in the district over which the County Council have jurisdiction, and therefore could not assent to the Corporation taking over the present order so far as it affects the portion of railway within the County, but that the County Council would be willing to join in a scheme for the reconstruction of the proposed Light Railway and provide the portion of the railway within their district, and arrange for the working of it in connection with the portion in the City."

The County Council seem to have dropped a bombshell soon after as a further report of the Tramways Committee states that: "without regarding the interests and convenience of the citizens and owners

*The late S. Pitcher.*

Nos. 2 and 4 on test at Tuffley.

96

and occupiers of property between the City and Brockworth, the County Council intend to support a proposal that Mr. Nevins (of the Cheltenham & District Light Railway) should be allowed to make a branch from Brockworth to the City in order to induce him to make the suggested line from Stroud to Cheltenham; but lest the scheme of Mr. Nevins should fall through, the County Council intend to apply for an Order empowering them to construct and work a Light Railway between The Cross Hands at Brockworth and the City Boundary."

The City Authorities considered an independent railway most unreasonable and foresaw inconvenience and waste of time by passengers changing and waiting for cars and " as there would be only a single line with occasional passing places, it would not be practicable to avoid that difficulty by arranging for running powers from the one railway to the other." They were even more against a branch from the Cheltenham line " having regard to the experience of Mr. Nevins' line between Cheltenham and Cleeve, the Corporation would not undertake to maintain, nor care to work a line so constructed. Moreover, the Corporation would not be content for the traffic to and from the City to be dependent on a supply of electricity from the Cheltenham Works, which have not been a success, and it is believed that on more than one occasion there has been a failure of the power."

The purchase price of the Horse Tramways was finally agreed at £26,000, and the transfer took place on 30th September, 1902. The company, however, continued to operate the services on the Corporation's behalf for a further three months, and the system did not, therefore, come fully under Municipal control until 1st January, 1903.

On 9th November, 1903, an interesting little ceremony was witnessed in the Bristol Road opposite the Wagon Works. This consisted of lifting the first of the rails of the old track, and the lowering of the first rail for the new one. The lifting was done by the retiring Mayor and the lowering by his successor. After that the last through car ran taking the Mayor and Corporation from this ceremony back to the Guildhall. Horse car services were gradually withdrawn as the electrification progressed, until on 17th March, 1904, the last horse tram ran, after giving 25 years' service.

## Electric Tramways.

The system constructed by the Corporation comprised the whole of the horse tramway system together with the authorised extensions to Cemetery Road, Stroud Road (with a short extension from Tuffley Avenue to Reservoir Road), Westgate Bridge, with a short extension over the bridge (4 furlongs 6 chains), a new section from Barton

Street to Tredworth via Parkend Road and to Churchdown Lane, Hucclecote, but not to The Cross Hands at Brockworth, making a total route mileage of 8 miles 7 furlongs 6½ chains. As a result of the disputes over the County portion of the railway the Light Railway Commissioners issued a separate order to the County Council authorising it to construct the line between Wotton and Hucclecote. In order to avoid unnecessary complication, it was further agreed that the line should be operated by the Corporation, at its own risk, under a 99 years' lease, with an option to purchase outright after 30 years, and recurring every seventh year thereafter. The Corporation was to bear the whole of the annual charge on the capital cost of construction, and in addition pay an annual wayleave of £50 in acknowledgment of County Council rights. It is of interest to note that this line was the only County-owned tramway outside the London area.

The work of reconstruction was carried on at good speed, personally superintended by the City Surveyor and his assistant, and the electrical installation was supervised by the new General Manager. The first trial car ran on 5th April, 1904. After the system had been approved by the Board of Trade Inspector, with the exception of the safety arrangements at Barton Gates, where the main line of the Midland Railway was crossed on the level, the system was formally opened by the Mayor on 7th May, 1904.

" The opening car was decorated with the City crest, etc., and 500 varicoloured incandescents, and the interior was decorated with taste and effect by Mr. Edwards' depot staff. A second car was also used but not so lavishly decorated. After lunch the Mayor of Cheltenham proposed the toast of the G.C.L.R. coupled with the name of the Mayor of Gloucester and the Tramways Committee. The Mayor of Gloucester was presented with a pair of silver mounted controllers, and a pair was also presented to Mr. Fream who drove the second car." The Mayor (who apparently had been having some driving practice the previous day) then drove off from outside the Guildhall into Northgate Street, and after exercising " due caution through the crowded streets . . . an excellent turn of speed was exhibited . . . three miles being covered in 20 minutes." After reversing at Hucclecote the party returned to the Sudbrook crossing, reversed and returned to the Guildhall and the Mayor declared the system open.

The illuminated car went out to Hucclecote and back " at a late hour. It glided, a veritable chariot of fire into the zone of darkness on the county road beyond Barnwood Bridge."

Returns for the first week of operation showed that the nine to ten cars in use ran 5,886 miles and carried 68,689 passengers, revenue being

£281 4s. 7d. (i.e. 11.46 pence per car mile run). By 21st June there were 14 cars in service and 81,000 passengers had been carried.

During the 1914-18 war an aerodrome and aircraft works were built at Brockworth, and it was decided to extend the Hucclecote route to serve this establishment, for both passengers and goods. War conditions, however, made it almost impossible to obtain the necessary materials, and it was therefore decided to take up the Westgate Street section (which carried but little traffic except at Barton Fair times) and to use the track and overhead equipment for the new extension. The Westgate Bridge section was therefore closed for a second time on 12th August, 1917, and the Brockworth line was opened for works traffic later in the same year. At the same time a siding was laid in from the Great Western Railway Goods Yard to a junction with the main line in London Road opposite Alvin Street, this being used for the collection by tram of all goods arriving for the aircraft works.* Some quite exceptional loads were carried this way. These extensions were constructed under the Defence of the Realm Act. The Brockworth extension carried some 1,200-1,300 workpeople per day in morning and evening journeys, but after the war it fell largely into disuse and was used only occasionally for goods traffic until the summer of 1922, when a regular public passenger service to the Victoria Hotel, Brockworth, was started. Traffic was still meagre, however, and the extension was abandoned entirely on 1st October, 1924, and the track was lifted soon afterwards.

On the main system the Stroud Road Junction - Tredworth Junction section was closed in 1927 (the only regular cars to use it in later years were workmen's cars from the Gloucester Railway Carriage & Wagon Co. works at lunch time, and cars coming off the Tuffley route at night, which could thus avoid the Cross). More widespread abandonment took place in September, 1929, when the Cemetery Road, Tuffley and Kingsholm routes were replaced by municipal buses. The remaining route, Bristol Road (Tuffley Avenue) to Hucclecote survived until 11th January, 1933, when the change over to buses was completed. The Corporation bus undertaking was subsequently taken over by the Bristol Tramways and Carriage Co., Ltd.

### SERVICES AND FARES.

At the opening, services were operated:
Tuffley Avenue and Hucclecote. Every 20 minutes 4.45 a.m. to 7.25 a.m. and 6.25 p.m. to 10.45 p.m. and every 15 minutes, 7.25 a.m. to 6.25 p.m. Through fare 3d.
Reservoir Road and City Boundary via Southgate Street. At the same frequencies as above. Fare 2d.

*No. 14 had the glass removed and was kept for this purpose.

Cemetery Road and Westgate Bridge. Same intervals. Through fare 1½d.

Reservoir Road and Kingsholm via Parkend Road. Same intervals. Through fare 2d.

Fare stages were ½d. for the first stage, 1d. for three stages, 1½d. for four stages, 2d. for six stages, 2½d. for seven stages and 3d. for eight stages.

Workmen's fares. Single two stages ½d., four stages 1d., six stages 1½d., seven stages 2d. and double for return.

There was some trouble at first with the Midland Railway with regard to the trams crossing their lines, and during the couple of months or so until this was settled, one car worked a shuttle service from Cemetery Road to Barton Gates.

Within a few years the services were altered to:

Cemetery Road - Westgate Bridge.
Bristol Road - Hucclecote.
Bristol Road - Barnwood School (later Barnwood Bridge).
Tuffley - Cross via Parkend Road.
Tuffley - Kingsholm via Southgate Street.

By 1914 the Tuffley service was confined to the Parkend route and Kingsholm cars reversed at The Cross. A few years before closing, on Saturdays Kingsholm cars worked to Bristol Road. There were also short workings Bristol Road-Cross. Service numbers were never used.

Football specials were worked from all parts to the Kingsholme line, and cars used to stand on the inward line, the service car using the wrong line from the terminus to a crossover near the ground.

When Westgate Street was closed, as before, a few yards of track were left in, and the last cars to use this are believed to have been

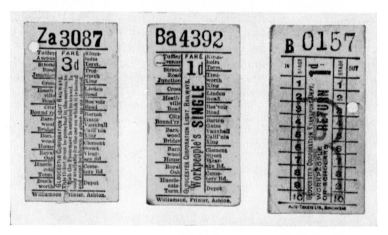

some evening specials run at the conclusion of the evening performances at the Three Choirs festival in 1920.

A tramways parcel service was operated for many years, the Receiving Office being situated at the Old Corn Exchange at The Cross.

The First Schedule of the Corporation Light Railway order quotes the rates to be charged:

" For every horse, mule or other beast of draught or burden, fourpence per head, per mile.

" For every ox, cow, bull, or head of cattle, threepence per head, per mile."

Other commodities specifically mentioned include coal, coke, chalk, lime, salt, etc., ironstone, iron ore, etc., heavy iron castings, earthenware, timber staves, deals, nails, anvils, vices, and chains, etc.

Carriages at 1/- per mile and bicycles 6d. for three miles, 2d. per three miles thereafter.

Parcels under 7 lb. 2d., and 7 to 14 lb. 4d.

Single articles of great weight not exceeding 2/- per ton per mile.

It is not thought that much use, if any, of these goods services was made!

## TICKETS.

No tickets were issued during the horse-tram days. The same type of ticket did duty for nearly the whole of this system's existence, and the colours remained the same, being 1d. pink, later becoming a more purplish shade, 1½d. green, 2d. blue till 1918 then violet, 2½d. white, 3d. yellow (3087), 3½d. salmon, 4d. greenish buff, 4½d. greyish buff. Workman return, white with red R on 1d., and blue R on 2d. Workman single 1d. value only, white (4392). Scholars return top half blue and lower half white. Exchanges were white with red X for 1d. and blue X for 2d. workmen's, and for scholars white and blue lower half and blue X on upper half. Till 1915 there was also a 1d. transfer, salmon with black skeleton letter overprint. Note that Brockworth is included on 3d. 3087 but not on the 1d. With the introduction of buses on some routes the title changed to Transport Dept. and numercial stage style tickets were issued. The colour scheme remained the same, but the printer was changed. 1d. W.Ret. 0157.

## ROLLING STOCK.

The rolling stock at first decided upon was 20 cars, but it was found that to run a five minute service, 30 cars would be required. A contract for 30 open-topped four-wheeled cars of conventional design, and one spare chassis, was therefore placed with the Brush Co. of Loughborough. They had four-window bodies seating 23/18 with plain wooden longitudinal seats in the lower deck and reversible garden seats on the upper deck arranged two and one. Overall length 25 ft., width 6 ft. 6 in., roof deck 9 ft. 8 in. above rail level. The truck was the standard Brush four-wheel rigid type with 6 ft. 6 in. wheelbase. They were equipped with Tidswell lifeguards.

All these cars were ultimately vestibuled, the screens being unglazed at the sides and having an ugly bulge at the bottom to clear the brake handle.

At first, cars carried the destination box high up, with a board to indicate if Tuffley cars were routed via Stroud Road. About 1920 this was lowered to a position over the driver's head, and side destination boards were introduced about the same time. For a short time an experiment in coloured destination rollers was tried, but was soon dropped.

There was also a water-sprinkler car (built on the spare chassis) consisting of a cylindrical tank with a canopy over. This car also acted as a rail grinder. There were also a number of four-wheeled

*Courtesy Mrs. Hyett.*
Car in grey livery, partly vestibuled and with side destination boards.

goods wagons, a truck containing welding equipment and a " mobile watchman's hut." These were built in the Corporation shops for the Brockworth extension. All the cars were eventually sold for scrap by public tender to a Newport (Mon.) firm where it is believed the trucks continued to give service to a colliery. No bodies are known to be still in existence.

The bodies of two horse trams, still in a good state of preservation exist in the garden of a house near the Pilot Bridge. Over each door is the following:

" Please observe that the Conductor ENTERS ON HIS WAY BILL each person received on the Car," with a hand pointing to a rack labelled Conductor's Way Bill Rear end of Car.

## LIVERY.

The original colours were crimson lake and cream, but in 1915, as a wartime measure, this was replaced by plain grey. This colour remained in use, however, until the closing of the system, and the lake and cream was not seen again on the Gloucester streets until it was carried by the municipal buses.

## TRACK.

The system was laid to the 3 ft. 6 in. gauge and totalled 15 track miles. The rails weighed 90 lb. per yard and were laid with the bars every 8 ft. on six inches of concrete paved with granite sets from Caernarvon, except in the city centre, where Australian Jarrah blocks were used. All points were 8 ft. 8 in. in length and all crossing work was supplied by Edgar Allen & Co., Ltd., Sheffield.

Double track extended from the Bristol Road terminus to the City Boundary at Wotton with a few yards of single track at Stroud Road Junction over the railway, over the Cross, and for about 250 yards in London Road. Double track also extended from Stroud Road Junction to the Tuffley terminus and from the Northgate Street Junction to the Kingsholm terminus; the latter section was singled in 1922/3 with one loop, after which inward cars joined the wrong road in Northgate Street, and used a crossover which was specially installed. Westgate Street was double tracked to just beyond St. Nicholas Church, and again over Westgate Bridge terminating in a crossover. There was a siding on the South side of the track on the City side of the bridge where the water car pulled in to fill from the river. (When the Westgate Street section was closed, this was filled from a standpipe at the depot.) Cemetery Road and Parkend Road sections were single line and loops. The County section was double for the first quarter mile and then single with eight passing loops.

There was a lamp signal at Barton Gates which showed a white light when a car from Tuffley entered the single line.

Temporary signals were installed in Lower Westgate Station during Barton Fair periods, and also on one occasion on the Brockworth extension.

The Hucclecote - Brockworth extension was laid on private right of way along the North side of the road, and included a loop and two spurs into the aerodrome works. (Some of the track can still be seen in the aerodrome approach where it serves as a footpath.)* The reserved track spur into the G.W. Rly. goods yard was laid with flat bottom rails on a disused pavement.

At three points, namely, Parkend Road (California Crossing), Barton Street and near Stroud Road Junction (Sudbrook Crossing) the tram lines were crossed on the level by lines of the late Midland Railway; the first was a single track and the other two were double lines, the tram track being single in each case. The tram track at California Crossing crossed the road on an S bend so as to cross the railway lines at right angles. Small semaphore signals mounted on a standard were installed to protect the trams on the City side of Sudbrook crossing, the outer side of Barton Gates crossing and both sides of California crossing. Catch points were also fixed in Southgate Street. The trackwork at these crossings was designed by the City Surveyor to the approval of the Midland Railway. It is interesting to note that *every* route went either over or under a railway, in some cases more than once.

The maximum gradient was 1 in 23 on the approaches to Barnwood Bridge, and the sharpest curve had a 40 ft. radius.

When the system was closed the track on the city side of Sudbrook Crossing, Barton Street, Eastgate Street, and Northgate Street was lifted, the rest being buried, though that from the City Boundary to Hucclecote was subsequently lifted when the road was widened and improved.

In addition to the crossovers mentioned, there were others outside the depot, near the Infirmary, Heathville Road, Wotton, Tredworth and at Linden Road.

The track generally was in very good condition and gave smooth riding. The original layout at the Cross gave curves round each of the four sides, but in 1921 this was relaid, the short section in Westgate Street being removed and curves to Eastgate Street only were left.

### CURRENT COLLECTION.

The system worked at 500 volts on overhead trolley with Dickenson's patent swivel head. Suspension was originally almost entirely

*This was covered during 1951.

Tuffley car with experimental route boards in use.

by side pole and bracket, using arms varying in length from 7 ft. 6 in. to 15 ft., and span wire was employed in a few places only. The wire was of O gauge with mechanical ears and earthed guard wires of galvanised steel. Every fifth pole was bonded to the rails and the overhead line was divided into the usual half-mile sections, the section boxes being fitted with telephones. The original frogs were of the pull-off type, but later automatic frogs with drop arms were installed at Barton Street, Stroud Road Junction and in Northgate Street, though the latter was later removed. When cars ceased to run from Eastgate Street to Northgate Street the wires on the curve were removed. For some time after the lines to Westgate Street had been removed the crossings remained in the overhead. During the 1914-18 war span wire was erected on streets where there were standards opposite and suitable, and the wires were suspended over the centre of the tracks except at bridges where side brackets were still employed. Later still the wires were moved to a position between the up and down tracks. There were no automatic trolley reversers, the trolley being turned by a bamboo pole slung alongside the car. Many standards are still in use for street lighting.

### DEPOT.

The depot was the later horse depot suitably enlarged and was situate in Bristol Road. It contained six roads with pits and could accommodate 50 cars. Provision was made for smithy and general repairs, as well as painting, to be carried out. The premises are now in use as a factory.

*   *   *

For the benefit of those exploring the traces, it may be added that the Tramway Junction signal box outside Gloucester Station has no bearing on the Corporation tramways but perpetuates the crossing of the Birmingham and Gloucester Railway by the Gloucester & Cheltenham Tramway, a horse worked mineral plateway.

*The late S. P. Tucker.*
The water sprinkler in London Road.

# THE LYNTON AND LYNMOUTH CLIFF RAILWAY

As reference has been made in this book to the Clifton Rocks Railway at Bristol and the Babbacombe Cliff Railway at Torquay, it is desirable, for the sake of completeness, to say something of the Lynton and Lynmouth line, for although, unlike these others, it has no association with a street tramway undertaking, it is the only line of " tramway " persuasion to have been constructed in the extensive area of North Devon.

The line owes its existence to the late Sir George Newnes, Bt., who sponsored the Clifton Rocks Railway and other similar projects and was also associated with the Lynton & Barnstaple Light Railway. It was opened on the 7th April, 1890, and is still at work. With a length of 901 feet, it is the longest of the British Cliff funiculars and to accommodate the two 3 ft. 6 in. gauge tracks, a cutting was excava-

The cars have lately been rebuilt with raised ends for observation and in this new state are fixed permanently to chassis.

*Block courtesy ' Railway Magazine.' Photo D. W. Winkworth.*
Descending car.

ted out of the cliff at an angle to the sea, ascending at 1 in 1¾ from Lynmouth Esplanade to a station near Lynton Town Hall approached from the main street by a narrow winding roadway. By virtue of weathering of the stone and the planting of many trees and shrubs to conceal much of the rock that was exposed, the railway far from being a disfigurement, is most attractive and harmonises easily with its beautiful surroundings.

A copious natural supply of water from the West Lyn river is used for traction purposes and the line worked on the hydraulic counterbalance system, the method of which will no doubt be familiar to readers. As a result of improvements made to the storage tanks

in 1923, it is possible for the ballast tank in the top car to be filled and the bottom one emptied in the same time taken for passenger turn-round, so that at the height of the summer season a continuous service can be operated.

The cars are individually controlled by brakesmen, a hydraulic service brake mounted on the end platform and a governor-controlled emergency brake being provided on each car. The twin steel haulage ropes connecting the upper ends of the cars are tested to a breaking strain of 50 tons and are supplemented by tail ropes to steady the cars in motion.

The car bodies, which were constructed locally, are mounted on the triangular type of undercarriage usually employed on cliff tramways but are unique in that they are detachable from the platform. They are, in fact, themselves carried on small flanged wheels and run on or off along a light rail track forming part of the platform. A similar track leads from the bottom station to a small car shed where the bodies are taken for painting and maintenance. The use of this method enables the carriages themselves to be used for transporting goods and light vehicles if and when required. The cars seat 16 persons on longitudinal seats and are of distinctly " tramcar " pattern. They are finished externally in green picked out in black, with a white roof.

Contrary to the usual practice on lines of this type, tickets are issued by the drivers, who carry a punch and rack in the approved style and combine fare collection with their braking duties. The fares are 3d. up and 2d. down, children being charged 1d. in either direction; the return fare is 5d. The service operates from June to September, commencing always at 8 a.m. and closing at 8 p.m. in June, 8.30 in July and 9 p.m. in August and early September.

The style of ticket and fares have remained more or less unchanged. In early days roll type tickets (0940) were issued and later Bell Punch tickets in packets were used (4115). Colours are 1d. child white, 2d. down pink, and 3d. up blue. Returns are *printed* in red (down) and blue (up) to denote direction.

It should be added that until 1923 there was an intermediate halt at North Walk, the halfway point, where the tracks are splayed out to allow the cars to pass one another. This, however, was eliminated in order to speed up the service.

The line is owned by the Lynmouth and Lynton Lift Company, of which Mr. E. Doe is Secretary and Mr. W. H. Jones, Engineer.

# PLYMOUTH

Prior to 1915, the Plymouth area was served by three separate electric tramway undertakings, namely Plymouth Corporation Tramways, which had its origin in an earlier horse and steam undertaking; the Devonport & District Tramways Co., Ltd., a B.E.T. subsidiary owning part of its system and leasing the rest from the Devonport Corporation; and the Plymouth, Stonehouse & Devonport Tramways Co., Ltd., which also began life as a horse-car line. All three systems continued to operate independently until 1915, when Plymouth extended its municipal boundary to take in the whole of Devonport and the urban district of East Stonehouse, and as that part of the Devonport & District system which was leased from the local corporation passed into Plymouth Corporation ownership, the company sold out completely to the corporation. Seven years later, the Plymouth, Stonehouse & Devonport system was acquired upon the expiry of its lease, and the whole of the tramways in the area thus became unified under the sole ownership and control of Plymouth Corporation.

It may readily be imagined that the existence within one urban area of three separate systems had many disadvantages and people living in Devonport suburbs, for example, were put to the inconvenience of changing cars, sometimes more than once, in order to reach the centre of Plymouth. The position was further aggravated by the unco-operative attitude adopted towards the two companies by the Plymouth Corporation, who had persistently refused to allow the operation of through services, even though there was no reason why this could not have been easily accomplished. The result of this state of affairs was that the system as a whole developed into a somewhat scattered collection of routes, several of which were unnecessarily devious and carried relatively little traffic, and although the corporation endeavoured to improve matters after the unification by constructing a new direct line into Devonport via Alma Road, the redundancy of many of the routes led to early abandonment in favour of motor buses.

## (i) PLYMOUTH, STONEHOUSE & DEVONPORT TRAMWAYS CO., LTD.

This was the oldest of the three undertakings mentioned, having been formed in 1870, and was the first system to be incorporated under the well-known and important (if unfortunate!) Tramways

Act passed in that year. The line was opened with horse trams on the standard (4 ft. 8½ in.) gauge on 17th March, 1872, when a trial service was run and passengers were carried free of charge. Regular operation commenced on the following day, the line then being 1 mile 74 chains in length and extending from Plymouth Clock Tower to Cumberland Road, Devonport, passing through a populous dockside district. In the same year as the opening, the company became a subsidiary of the Provincial Tramways Co., Ltd., a holding concern notable for its activities in Portsmouth. An extension authorised in 1874 carried the trams into the heart of Devonport, proceeding by a one-way arrangement (inwards along Chapel Street and outwards via Albyn Street) and terminating in Fore Street at the foot of Marlborough Street. This increased the length of the line to 2½ miles, and in his 'Tramways, their Construction and Working,' volume 2, 1881, D. K. Clarke gives the following figures in respect of its operation for the year ended 30th June, 1880:

Gross receipts ... ... £8,888. Net profit £1,504.
Working expenses ... £7,384.
Passengers carried ... 1,074,346.
Car miles run ... ... 134,724.
Rolling stock ... ... 8 cars and 78 horses.

These earlier cars had knifeboard seats outside, but the later ones had " garden " seats and were larger. In 1895 the company had

*Courtesy R. C. Sambourne.*
Plymouth, Stonehouse and Devonport No. 4.

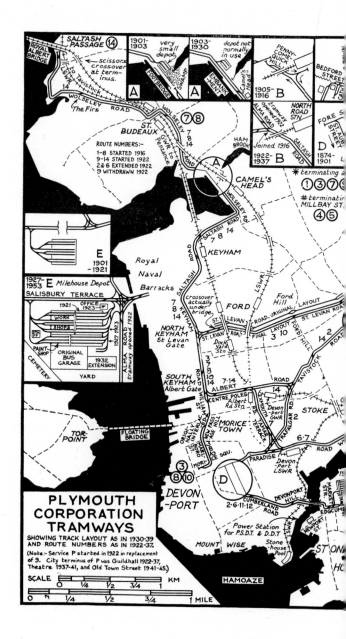

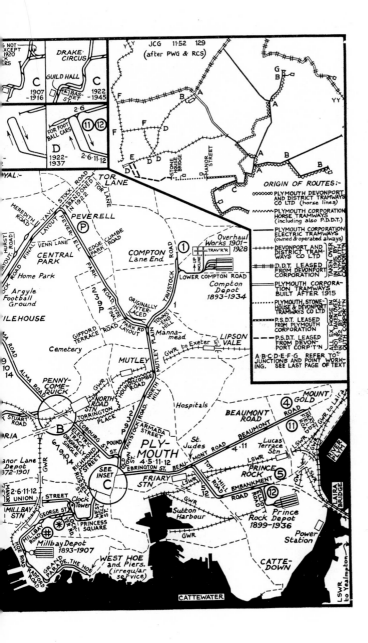

12 cars and 116 horses and the depot and the stables were situate in Manor Lane, Stonehouse; these premises are still in existence and are used as a garage. The cars were normally drawn by two horses but three extra ones were attached for taking them up Devonport Hill, from Stonehouse Bridge to Mount Wise. Incidentally, Stonehouse Bridge (known locally as Ha'penny Bridge) was a toll bridge and remained so until the 1st April, 1924.

In 1901, the track in the boroughs of Plymouth and Devonport was sold to the respective corporations and only the section in Stonehouse, between Edgcumbe Street and Manor Street, remained under the company's ownership. At the same time the line was relaid to the 3 ft. 6 in. gauge and electrified on the overhead trolley system, and electrical operation commenced on 18th November, 1901. The company continued to operate the section of line which had been sold to the municipalities under a 21 years' lease.

The original electric rolling stock comprised 15 double-deck opentop cars of the conventional balcony type with three side windows and reversed stairs. These were numbered 1-12 and 14-15, there being no car numbered 13 (Exeter's avoidance of that sinister number

*Courtesy R. C. Sambourne.*
Plymouth, Stonehouse & Devonport No. 11 in Fore Street, Devonport. Note destination board in front and advertisement on side board.

would seem to indicate that superstition was rife in Devon in those days!) Later, No. 16 was added and this car differed only in having normal stairs. The cars seated 24 passengers inside and a like number on top, and were mounted on Brill 21E trucks with Dick, Kerr equipment. The indicators consisted of a board fitted in front of the controls at either end of the car and showing PLYMOUTH or DEVONPORT, and the fleet colours were light green and cream with a belt and buckle device surrounding the car number on the waist panel and the company's full title emblazoned on the rocker. The cars were housed in a new depot at the corner of Market Street and Edgcumbe Street, Stonehouse, which had six roads capable of holding 18 cars, although, of course, there were only 15 to go in! A traverser provided the only access to roads 4-6.

The method of working included two rather unusual features. One was that standing passengers (limited to six inside) were only allowed after passing Edgcumbe Street eastbound and as far as that stage westbound, this being on account of Devonport Hill, which, although not unduly steep, was the scene of one major accident. Secondly, the fares differed according to whether one travelled on the upper or lower deck, the through fare, for instance, being 2d. inside and only 1½d. on top.

Between the Clock Tower and Manor Street, Plymouth Corporation supplied power from its own generating station and the overhead suspension was of the standard P.C.T. design (to be described later). Power for the rest of the line was taken from the Devonport Corporation installation in Newport Street, Stonehouse, and the overhead on this section was of the orthodox single side pole and bracket type with the crests of Devonport Corporation and East Stonehouse U.D.C. on the pole bases in the respective areas. An exception was over Stonehouse Bridge, where centre poles were used. The track was single-and-loop through Stonehouse but double elsewhere, and the one-way working into Devonport was reversed upon electrification so that the two tracks no longer crossed; it must also be mentioned that the terminal spur in Fore Street was not electrified at this time, the track which did exist there many years later not being laid in until after 1922. The track was entirely in streets and laid with rails weighing 84 lb. per yard. The sharpest curve had a radius of 34 feet and the maximum gradient (Devonport Hill) was 1 in 11.

## (ii) DEVONPORT & DISTRICT TRAMWAYS CO., LTD.

This undertaking was opened on the 26th June, 1901, and operated electrically from the outset. The lines constructed by the company extended from Morice Square to the Camel's Head, Saltash Road;

Fore Street to Pennycomequick (Stuart Road) via Paradise Road; Paradise Road to Milehouse via Trafalgar Road and Tavistock Road; South Keyham to Trafalgar Road via Albert Road; and Albert Road to Paradise Road via Tamar Terrace. These sections totalled 4.75 route miles.

Meanwhile, in 1900, Devonport Corporation had secured powers to construct and operate tramways from the Camel's Head to St. Budeaux and Saltash Passage and from North Keyham to Tor Lane, Peverell, via St. Levan's Road and the upper part of Tavistock Road, a total of 3 miles 45 chains. The two lines being disconnected and virtually tacked on to the existing company system, the corporation later decided not to operate the lines themselves and upon completion these were handed over to the Devonport & District Tramways Co., Ltd., to be worked under lease. Prior to 1903, the section from Camel's Head to St. Budeaux was completely isolated from the main system owing to an embankment being under construction, and two cars (Nos. 22 and 24) maintained a shuttle service between those points, the respective railheads at the Camel's Head being connected by a temporary wooden bridge.

The services were operated thus:
Fore Street - Tor Lane via Tavistock Road.
Fore Street - Stuart Road via Wilton Street.
South Keyham - Stuart Road via Tamar Terrace (extended when required to St. Budeaux and Saltash).
Morice Square - St. Budeaux - Saltash Passage.
Morice Square - Tor Lane via Fordhill.

The company's rules and regulations for motormen and conductors contained several instructions which appear very quaint when compared to present-day practice, of which the following, quoted from the general regulations, are especially comical:

" Motormen and conductors . . . should be attentive to duty, carefully observing every person as they proceed along the streets, and if they notice anyone standing looking at the cars, undecided whether or not to ride, make a motion with their hands to attract their attention, which would many times induce them to ride, and thereby increase the business of the company.

" They must, when standing at a terminus, and when approaching intending passengers, announce in a clear and distinct tone of voice, the route and destination of their car.

" Disparaging remarks by the employees about the management of the routes, or about the officers of the company, will not be allowed, and will be regarded as a breach of the rules.

" They must not enter into unnecessary conversation with the

*Courtesy R. C. Sambourne.*
Devonport & District No. 4, American built class, at Pennycomequick.
Note separate slipper brake wheel. (The boy is leaning on it.)

passengers, nor make signs, motions or signals of any kind to
men in charge of other cars."

The company owned 33 cars, all open-top four-wheelers of which
the first batch (Nos. 1-20) were of the uncanopied type and built by
the J. G. Brill Car Co. in the U.S.A. They had three curved-top
windows per side and direct quarter-turn stairs. They were fitted
with mechanical track brakes worked by a separate wheel on the nearside of the controller. Nos. 21-25 were of the same type but were
constructed in this country by Brush and had five rectangular side
windows and the conventional type of slipper brake. The
next four cars, Nos. 26-29, were of the balcony pattern with normal
stairs and four side windows, while Nos. 30-33 were similar but had
reversed stairs.* All the cars were fitted with roller blind indicators
mounted at a considerable height above the guard rails and had the
headlamps on the canopies; the appearance of a circular metal plate
fitted over the normal dash light position in photographs of cars of

*These cars were obtained from City of Birmingham Tramways Co. prior
to its purchase by the Corporation *circa* 1912.

the first two series suggests that the lamps were removed to the upper position at a later date, and, in fact, the headlamps on the Brill cars were removed entirely during the first World War. Coloured lights were also used for route indication by night.

The company's livery was originally chocolate and cream with the magnet and wheel device of the B.E.T. group displayed on the waist panel, but a change to green and cream was under way when the system was acquired by Plymouth. Advertisements were carried, and these were even affixed on the seat backs and stair risers! The main

*Courtesy R. C. Sambourne.*
Devonport & District No. 21 at St. Budeaux. Note repositioned headlamp and adverts on stair risers.

depot was located at Milehouse, and there was also a crude corrugated-iron shed at Camel's Head with two roads holding one car each; this latter was erected for the cars which shuttled to and from Saltash before that section was linked with the main system and thereafter was only used for housing damaged or defective cars. The current supply was drawn from the Devonport Corporation power house at Stonehouse Creek.

The track was of 3 ft. 6 in. gauge, and that constructed by the company was double throughout with the exception of one length of interlaced track in William Street between South Keyham Gates and the foot of New Passage Hill, while the sections leased from the corporation included one of single-and-loop track in St. Levan's Road and along Tavistock Road to Meredith Road, but were otherwise double. The rails used throughout were of 97 lb. section, the sharpest curve being 50 ft. radius, and there was no reserved track. The maximum gradient was 1 in 10 in Tamer Terrace, whereon there were two fatal accidents, both of which occurred in 1902 and involved cars of the 21-25 (Brush) series. On the morning of the 3rd June, No. 25, full of dockyard men returning from night shift, ran away down the hill and came to grief at the bottom, causing the death of one passenger, while on the 27th September another car likewise got out of control and, jumping the track at the junction of Paradise Road, ran into the wall at the entrance to the L. & S.W.R. station, one man being killed and several injured. In each case, the slipper brakes failed to check the car.

Overhead construction was of the usual side pole and bracket type with both wires upheld by the same bracket, except between the bottom of Albert Road and the junction of Exmouth Road, where centre poles were used; span wire was employed only at junctions and depots.

### (iii) PLYMOUTH CORPORATION (1880-1915).

In 1880, the Plymouth, Devonport & District Tramways Co., Ltd., was incorporated with powers to construct and operate several lines of tramway in both towns, the use of mechanical traction being permitted. The company duly proceeded with certain of the authorised routes in Plymouth, where they regarded the potential traffic as more lucrative, but took no action with regard to the lines in Devonport. The latter corporation, therefore, took the matter to court and obtained an injunction prohibiting the company from working its lines in Plymouth until such time as it had constructed those in Devonport. This the company were unable to do owing to lack of the necessary capital and the undertaking therefore collapsed. Exactly how much

Plymouth Corporation horse tram.

actual operation the company carried out in Plymouth has not been determined, but it is known that they laid lines to Mannamead, Millbay and North Road and ran a meagre service with the aid of five Wilkinson vertical-boiler steam engines in 1884/85.*

After the steam cars were withdrawn in 1885 another company was formed under the name Plymouth Tramways Company, and it operated horse trams over the steam lines. This company was purchased by the corporation in 1892. The cars were painted red and cream with the name in full on the lower rocker panel and coat of arms on the upper.

Then, in 1892, Plymouth Corporation took the matter into its own hands and acquired the company's property for £12,500. It then proceeded to construct the routes previously authorised and opened them with horse traction as follows:

| | |
|---|---|
| Millbay and West Hoe ... | 11th March, 1893. |
| Compton Lane End ... | 3rd April, 1893. |
| Prince Rock ... ... | 10th December, 1896. |

In 1894 the line from Coburg Street was extended to Market Avenue via Tavistock Road and Old Town Street and the service along Richmond Street, Russell Street and Bedford Street was withdrawn and the lines taken up, thus leaving the service Westwell Street

*These were later sold to a works at Swanscombe, Kent, and operated there until 1922.

to West Hoe isolated. This was operated with single deck cars, one horse per car. In 1895 a direct line was laid from Mutley Plain to Market Avenue via Tavistock Road, Tavistock Place and Old Town Street; these services continued till electrification.

The horse-cars seated 12 passengers inside and the same number on top and were housed in depots at Compton Lane End and Millbay. The journey from Compton into town in those days took 20 minutes and cost one penny. The rolling stock during the final years of the horse tramways totalled 47 cars and 127 horses, but the services provided still fell short of the required standard and in 1898 the corporation obtained powers to electrify the system and build additional routes.

Work commenced at once, the contractors being the Electric Construction Company, and the first electric car, duly beflagged for the occasion, was driven from Prince Rock to the Theatre on the 22nd September, 1899. Other routes were opened in the following order:

| | |
|---|---|
| Compton ... ... ... | 4th April, 1901. |
| Beaumont Road ... ... | 2nd April, 1902. |
| Peverill via Mutley ... ... | 13th January, 1905. |
| Pennycomequick via North Road | 21st September, 1905. |
| West Hoe ... ... ... | 22nd June, 1907. |

These sections amounted to 6 miles 35 chains in length. During its reconstruction, the Compton route was laid partly over a different course to the original horse tramway, which had followed a circuitous " back street " route; two sections of old line were abandoned, namely those along Russell Street and Richmond Street, between Bedford Street and Cobourg Street, and along Torrington Place and Houndiscombe Road, the latter section being replaced by a direct line along Tavistock Road.* The intervening section in Cobourg Street was subsequently utilised for the Pennycomequick route.

SERVICES AND FARES.

1. Theatre - Mutley - Compton.
2. Theatre - Mutley - Peverell.
3. West Hoe - Drake Circus - North Road Station (Pennycomequick).
4. Theatre - Drake Circus - Beaumont Road.
5. Theatre - Drake Circus - Prince Rock.

Originally, the services were not numbered, but were indicated by coloured discs attached to the car dashboards in addition to roller blind indicators. Later, the coloured signs were replaced by numbered discs.

In 1905, the Beaumont Road service was extended down Union

*Not to be confused with Tavistock Road, Devonport.

Street to Manor Street, over the track leased to the P.S. & D. Co., but this was short-lived and the service reverted to the Theatre. Later, it was again extended to Millbay Station, also running to the Hoe when required, and the West Hoe-North Road service was then curtailed at the Theatre. From that time onwards, there was no regular service to the Hoe, which was covered by extensions of other services when necessary.

Representative fares at this time were: ½d. for West Hoe - Theatre, Theatre - Drake Circus; 1d. for Theatre - Hyde Park, Theatre - North Road Station; 1½d. for Theatre - Peverell and Compton; and 2d. for Manor Street - Beaumont Road and Prince Rock.

This tariff was replaced by a universal penny fare in 1914.

### ROLLING STOCK.

The corporation's fleet totalled 55 cars by the end of 1915, all of which were four-wheeled. Nos. 1-6 were supplied in 1899 for the opening of the system and were uncanopied cars with four curved-top windows per side, 42 seats and direct quarter-turn stairs, while 7-20, which followed in 1900, were a veranda balcony version of the same job fitted with reversed stairs. Both series were built by Brush and mounted on Peckham cantilever trucks with Westinghouse equipment. Nos. 2, 5, and 6 were later fitted with canopies (making them similar to the second batch), No. 5 at the same time acquiring reversed stairs. No. 15 was given conventional half-turn stairs and slipper brakes were gradually fitted to most of the cars. Also, No. 12 was re-trucked with a Brill 21E believed to have come from a Devonport car.

Car 12 was again re-trucked with a Brill 21E from one of the single-deckers 37-42. All these cars were scrapped in 1924 with the exception of 42 which became the welding car.

The next additions were Nos. 21-30 from Milnes in 1903; these were balcony cars with four rectangular side windows surmounted by half-lights, and had normal stairs (half-turn) and Peckham trucks of an improved design. Like the earlier cars, they had no headlamps. Nos. 31-36, delivered in 1905, were Brush-built balcony cars and showed a considerable advance on previous types.

Cars 21-30 were mounted on Peckham Cantilever Trucks: 27-30 on Brush Conalty trucks. 28 was later fitted with a round dash with headlamp.

Then came six single-deckers (37-42) supplied—again by Brush—in 1906 for the West Hoe - North Road Station service. These were very small cars designed and fitted for one-man operation and had a peculiar type of semi-vestibule, which, while affording protection for passengers seated on the platform, left the poor motorman at the

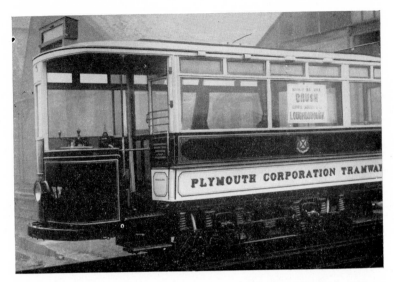

*Brush, courtesy R. Elliott.*
Single-deck demi-car as delivered by Brush.

*Courtesy P.C.T.*
Plymouth Corporation 7-20 class Brush cars on Peckham Cantilever trucks,
at theatre terminus.

*Courtesy P.C.T.*

No. 24 at Prince Rock.

mercy of the elements! They were 21 ft. 10 in. long over fenders, with 11 ft. 4 in. body, and were mounted on Brush 5 ft. 6 in. trucks.

Finally came 12 more balcony cars of Brush construction (Nos. 43-54), placed in service in 1915, and an open-sided rail grinder, which did not carry a number.

## LIVERY.

Bright red and yellow.

## TRACK.

The system had a total track length of 15 miles and was double with the exception of the West Hoe route, which was partly single-and-loop, and excluding also a single line in Cobourg Street, a length of interlaced track in Hyde Park Road from the junction with the Compton route to Plymouth College and another near the Guildhall. The rails weighed 92 lb. per yard and the gauge was 3 ft. 6 in. The maximum gradient was 1 in 9 and occurred in the climb up to North Road Station, while the sharpest curve had a radius of 35 ft.

There was a very curious arrangement at North Road Station at one time; the up line *only* was diverted into the station approach and having loaded for the town, cars then rejoined the main road after a second reversal. Another short piece of trackage not regularly used was the set of curves from Ebrington Street northwards into Old Town Street at Drake Circus; these were only used for a short time about 1920 for cars going to and from the dockyard.

## CURRENT COLLECTION.

The orthodox overhead trolley system was employed, with side pole and bracket arm suspension on all routes. Separate poles and brackets on either side of the road were provided for the up and down wires except between the Theatre and West Hoe, in Hyde Park Road, and from Friary Station to Prince Rock, on which sections a single pole and arm supported both wires. The undertaking supplied its own power from Prince Rock, a sub-station being erected at Armada Street, off Tavistock Road.

## DEPOTS.

These were two in number. The larger was Prince Rock, which housed 28 cars on four roads with the power house nearby, while Compton Depot had five roads in the yard and four in the shed, which held 16 cars and was the original horse-car depot converted. The former stables were turned into a store and the roof of the car shed itself had to be raised to take the overhead wiring. A third depot was a small one at Millbay holding about ten cars on four roads radiating, roundhouse-fashion, from a turntable, but this was not electrified. Millbay Depot was not used after 1907.

The depots were linked by the Tramways Department's private telephone system, the wires for which were attached to the tramway poles and also served several street call boxes located at important points for the use of regulators and crews.

## (iv) PLYMOUTH CORPORATION (1915-1945).

Upon the expansion of its boundaries to include Devonport, the Plymouth Corporation acquired the tramways of the Devonport & District Tramways Co., Ltd., and those which the latter leased from Devonport Corporation, on 2nd October, 1915. In the following year, a junction was laid in at Pennycomequick to connect the two systems and the long-needed through services into Devonport commenced in October, 1916. Further through travel facilities were then made possible by the construction of a new line along Alma Road, between Pennycomequick and Milehouse, which was opened on 1st June, 1922.

As its lease still had seven years to run, the Plymouth, Stonehouse & Devonport Tramways Co., Ltd., had been allowed to continue independently when the municipal merger had taken place, and it was

*Plymouth Corporation
Transport.*
No. 74 in yellow livery;
this was formerly a Devonport & District car.
One of the ex-P.S. & D.
cars as rebuilt by Plymouth
Corporation for single-end
operation on the circular
routes.

not until the lease expired on 1st July, 1922, that this undertaking was
purchased by the corporation, although it will be remembered that
that authority had owned the track within its area since 1901. Con-
nections were immediately laid in at Fore Street and two circular
services were instituted, running via Peverell, Milehouse and Union
Street and via Wilton Street and Union Street respectively.

Subsequent to the merger, the corporation had obtained powers for several tramway extensions, but the Alma Road line was the only one to materialise and with the completion of the curves into the ex-P.S. & D. line and a terminal spur in Fore Street for football specials, etc., the tramways reached their maximum route length of 17 miles 46 chains. Before 1930, however, the terminal spur at Tor Lane, Peverell, had been abandoned, and at about that time the system began to decline. Anxiety had for some time been felt about the condition of much of the track and rolling stock and also about the heavy loan debt which had existed ever since the construction of the tramways. Consideration was given to the possibility of trolleybus operation but eventually the corporation decided to adopt a ten-year programme of replacement of tramways by motor bus services. Routes were accordingly changed over in the following order:

| | |
|---|---|
| Morice Square - Saltash Passage ... | 27th October, 1930. |
| Theatre - West Hoe ... ... | 16th February, 1931. |
| Theatre - Beaumont Road ... ... | 19th October, 1931. |
| Theatre - Compton ... ... ... | 11th April, 1932. |
| Theatre - R.N. Barracks via Wilton Street (regular service) | 9th July, 1934. |
| Theatre - R.N. Barracks via Alma Road (regular service) | 9th July, 1934. |
| Milehouse - Fordhill - Devonport ... | 3rd June, 1935. |
| Drake Circus - Prince Rock ... | 23rd February, 1936. |
| Theatre - Wilton Street - Fore Street | 4th April, 1937. |
| Theatre - Theatre via Milehouse and Union Street ... ... ... | 9th May, 1937. |

A few weeks before service 8 was withdrawn, services 7 and 14 terminated at North Keyham, and passengers for St. Budeaux and Saltash Passage were transferred to service 8. Services 7 and 14 were extended to R.N. Barracks in August, 1931.

Despite these conversions (which left only the Guildhall - Mutley - Peverell section under regular operation) workmen's cars continued to operate between the Theatre and South and North Keyham via Wilton Street and via Alma Road and Tavistock Road (Devonport) until 25th March, 1939. Moreover, when the Bath & West Show was held in Central Park from 25th to 28th May, 1938, additional trams were operated to Fore Street via Peverell.

By the outbreak of war in September, 1939, the Theatre - Peverell section was still working and in view of motor fuel restrictions, this continued to operate for the duration of hostilities. The track from Peverell to Milehouse was also kept in commission so as to give access to the depot. The service was interrupted for about a month in March, 1941, owing to air-raid damage to the track and overhead, which was particularly severe in the inner part of the city and resulted in the tram service, on its resumption, being cut back from the Theatre to Old Town Street. The corporation even replaced fallen overhead on one or two disused sections which had been left intact after withdrawal of service, but no additional tram services were operated. The remaining one proved a boon to Plymouth people during the war but, unfortunately, in June, 1943, the City Council decided to abandon it as soon as sufficient buses became available.

The last Plymouth tram (No. 158), left Old Town Street for Peverell at 5 p.m. on Saturday, 29th September, 1945. It was decorated with union jacks and bunting and driven by Motorman H. Herring, the oldest employee on the tramways. The car carried 135 passengers on the last run and two conductors were required to handle this " outsize " load! Among those on board were the Traffic Superintendent of the undertaking and his deputy, also Mr. W. A. Smith, who had driven the first electric tram in 1899. Upon arrival at Milehouse Depot, the car was met by the Lord Mayor and other civic dignitaries and a tea was held in the Transport Department's canteen. During the speeches made, it was stated that in their 46 years of service, the trams carried some 800 million passengers and travelled over 70 million miles.

## SERVICES AND FARES.

Following upon the absorption of the company-operated tramways and the completion of the Alma Road link, the services were thoroughly reorganised and route number boxes were fitted to all cars. The universal penny fare in Plymouth was scrapped and a new fare tariff introduced, giving one stage for 1d., three stages for 1½d. and each additional stage a halfpenny up to a maximum of 4d. on the longest runs.

The full list of services as operative from 1923, with fares in brackets, was as under:

1. Theatre - Sherwell (1d.) - Hyde Park (1½d.) - Compton (1½d.).
2. Theatre - Hyde Park - Peverell (1½d.) - Milehouse (2d.) - Fore Street (3d.) - Theatre (4d.).
2a. Reverse of 2.
3. Theatre - Peverell - Milehouse - Ford Hill - North Keyham (2½d.) - Morice Square (3d.).
4. Beaumont Road - St. Jude's (1d.) - Drake Circus - Theatre (1½d.) - Millbay (1½d.).
5. Prince Rock - Drake Circus - Theatre - Millbay (1½d.).
6. Theatre - Pennycomequick (1d.) - Wilton Street (1½d.) - Fore Street (2d.) - Stonehouse - Theatre (3d.).
6a. Reverse of 6.

7. Theatre - Pennycomequick - Wilton Street - South Keyham (2d.) - Wolseley Road (2½d.) - St. Budeaux (3d.).
7a. Theatre - South Keyham.
8. Morice Square - North Keyham (1d.) - St. Budeaux (1½d.).
9. Theatre - Peverell - Milehouse - Alma Road - Theatre (3d.)
9a. Reverse of 9.
10. Theatre - Pennycomequick - Milehouse (1½d.) - North Keyham (1½d.) - Morice Square (2d.).
11. Beaumont Road - Theatre (1½d.) - Edgcumbe Street (2d.) - Fore Street (3d.).
12. Prince Rock - Theatre - Fore Street (3d.).
13. No service.
14. Theatre - Alma Road - Milehouse (1½d.) - South Keyham (2d.) - Wolseley Road (2½d.) - St. Budeaux (3d.) - Saltash Passage (4d.).
14a. Theatre - Milehouse - South Keyham.

There was still no regular service to the Hoe, routes 1, 3, 4, 5, 7 and 14 being extended there as and when required, and service 9 in summer. The 3d. single journeys on services 7, 11, 12 and 14 were 5d. return, and a sixpenny return was issued for the 4d. single journey from Theatre to Saltash (route 14). The average service frequency was 12 minutes, but certain routes had much thinner headways and ran without published timetables. Service 9 had been withdrawn by 1928 but part of it survived as Service P, operating between Guildhall and Peverell via Hyde Park. In 1937, the remaining tram routes were numbered in with the bus services, thus:

Services 9 and 9a were withdrawn in 1922 and part became P but only ran for about six months. P became 11 in 1937 but the then remaining cars did not carry this number. Services 1 and 2 were withdrawn on 9th May, 1937, and as from that day no cars ran on Sundays, the service being provided by buses.

On the withdrawal of 1 and 2, service 11 was extended from Guildhall to Theatre and it was, of course, this route (latterly curtailed at Old Town Street) which continued to operate through the war. In the 1945 timetables, it was running an eight-minute headway on weekdays only from 6.34 a.m. to 9.14 p.m. (inwards) and from 6.50 a.m. to 9.30 p.m. (outwards), at a flat fare of 1½d.

## TICKETS.

The tickets in this district underwent many changes in the early days, each route having separate colours. During the '20s it was somewhat stabilised to 1d. white, 1½d. purple, 2d. blue, 3d. orange, 4d. olive and 5d. pink. Child tickets were 1d. blue and 2d. green, while exchange tickets were buff with red E overprint. The illustra-

129

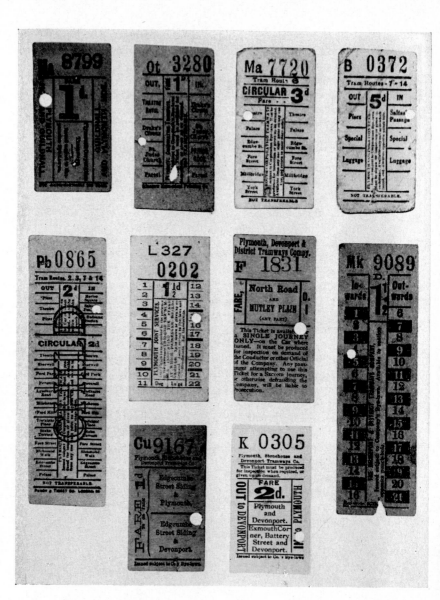

tions show 1d. blue 8799, a very early corporation ticket. 1d. blueish-green 3280, a later style by Glasgow Numerical Printing Co.; note the capital letters for the terminal points. At this time each route had a differently coloured penny ticket. 3d. yellow 7720 by Punch and Ticket Co. has identical stages on each side being for the full circular journey. 5d. pink 0372 issued by Plymouth corporation TRAMS shows the highest value issued. Note the addition of SPECIAL and LUGGAGE and blank spaces to fill up. 2d. child, green with red overprint 0865 covers a variety of routes and also the circular journey. 1½d. salmon 0202 issued on a tram during the last days (actually 21st May, 1945) is the type used on Plymouth corporation and Western National joint services. 1d. lilac 1831 is a very early example of the bell punch ticket, then a novelty, and was issued by the Plymouth, Devonport and District Tramways Company. 1d. greyish-purple 9167 and 2d. buff 0305 are examples of tickets issued on the Plymouth, Stonehouse and Devonport Tramways Co. 1½d. green 9089 issued by Devonport and District Tramways Co. is an example of the patented " Fair Fare " system.

## ROLLING STOCK.

The 33 cars taken over from the Devonport & District system in 1915 included a number that were unusable, and, for the time being, only 15 of them were renumbered, becoming Nos. 55-69 (the corporation's own numbering then ending at 54). Five of the American cars (1-20 series) and two of the Brush cars (believed to be Nos. 22 and 24) were scrapped, and the remaining 26 ex-Devonport cars, including the 15 previously renumbered, were allotted the Plymouth numbers 63-88 in the following manner: the 15 survivors of the 1-20 series became Nos. 74-88; Nos. 21/23/25 became 63-65; Nos. 26-29 became 66/69; and Nos. 30-33 became 70-73. Later still, Nos. 71 and 73 were yet again renumbered 41/2, and Nos. 75, 79 and 83 converted to single-deck permanent way cars; the last two of these had been fitted with canopies after being taken over, and other ex-Devonport cars likewise treated included No. 74.

In 1916/17, Brush supplied Nos. 55-62 (occupying numbers vacated by renumbered ex-Devonport cars) and also Nos. 94-105 in 1919/20; these were three-window balcony cars mounted on Peckham P.22 trucks. During the same period, the corporation itself constructed in the Milehouse works five new cars of generally similar design, in which many components of scrapped ex-Devonport cars were used; these were numbered 90-93 and 112, all being similar to the 55-62 batch except No. 93, which, by the resemblance of its bodywork to that of the Devonport 21-25 series, is thought to have contained even less new material than the others. The numbers 89 and 106-111 (and later 128-130) were left blank.

A further addition of 15 cars came with the acquisition of the Plymouth, Stonehouse & Devonport Tramways in 1922, and these cars became Nos. 113-127 in the P.C.T. fleet. Ten of them (Nos. 114-123) were rebuilt by the corporation for single-end operation on the

No. 147, built by English E'ectric Co., Ltd.

Right: Plymouth, Stonehouse & Devonport Tramways rebuilt for single ended operation on circular route.  On left: two ex-Exeter cars at Theatre.

circular routes 2, 2a, 6 and 6a, and in this condition they presented a curious appearance as only the driving end was vestibuled and stairs were fitted at the rear end only. Concurrently, Nos. 124-127 were rebuilt along more orthodox lines with double-end control, and later No. 119 was again rebuilt to conform with them. Car No. 113, which was formerly P.S. & D. No. 16, being newer than its fellows, was not altered.

In 1924, 20 new cars were delivered by the English Electric Co., Ltd., and numbered 131-150. In these, the open-top four-wheeled type was perpetuated but the cars were of a much improved design, being vestibuled and mounted on 21E 7 ft. 6 in. trucks giving much steadier riding. Moreover, Nos. 136, 139, 141, 142, 145, 146 and 148-150 were later fitted with leather upholstered transverse seats. On account of their angular appearance, these cars became known among the staff as " square faces." In the same year, the six demi-cars (Nos. 37-42) were withdrawn from service, but No. 42 was retained as a welding car.

The first bogie tram to run in Plymouth was No. 151, an experimental car constructed at Milehouse in 1925. It was vestibuled (although, unfortunately, still open-topped) and had upholstered seating on both decks and magnetic brakes. The car proved to be successful and a further 15, similar in appearance but of a much improved design (Nos. 152-166) were built by the corporation in 1927/8, these later models being fitted with air brakes as well as magnetic. English Electric equipment was used throughout and compressed-air bells were fitted. These bogie cars were very striking in appearance, particularly in comparison with the majority of the Plymouth rolling stock, and among the features which gave them a modern look may be mentioned the deep panelling and the twin head and tail lamps instead of the conventional single dashlight. It was found, however, that the bogie trucks were not well-suited to the sharp curvature and deteriorating condition of the track (particularly in Princess Square, where there were several derailments) and all 16 cars except Nos. 156, 163 and 164 later had their bogies replaced by long-wheelbase single trucks.

Upon the abandonment in 1931 of the Exeter tramways, Plymouth Corporation purchased nine of their vestibuled four-wheeled cars, which were given the numbers 1-9, while in 1933, six vestibuled bogie and six open-ended four-wheeled cars were acquired from the Torquay Tramways Co. Ex-Torquay cars 37-42 became 12 to 15 and 10 and 11, and 7, 9, 10, 16, 17 and 18 became 16-21. Nos 12-15 were notable for having roller bearings and upholstered longitudinal seating whereas 10 and 11 had upholstered transverse seating. These were the last trams to be purchased by the corporation. One of the early cars

*W. A. Camwell.*
No. 163 of the 1927 bogie series.

*D. W. Winkworth.*
No. 158 at Peverell on 2nd August, 1945; former bogie car on single truck.

(No. 22) was decorated for the " All Electric House " exhibition in April, 1931, and toured the city.

Although the numbering reached 166, the total number of cars in Plymouth at any one time never exceeded 127, since all the later additions were used to replace older stock. No top-covered trams were ever operated, and of the pre-1924 cars, none except the single-enders was ever vestibuled and only four (Nos. 45, 91, 100 and 101) were given upholstered seating. The standard of maintenance was generally rather low.

Thirteen cars (all of the ex-bogie type) were left to carry on the Theatre - Peverell service after 1939, these being Nos. 151-155, 157-162, 165 and 166. During the air raids in April, 1941, No. 153 was burned out in Basket Street, while No. 159 was seriously damaged and could not be used again. No. 158 was damaged in Tavistock Road but was repaired; with the other ten remaining cars it resumed the service from Drake Circus only and maintained it until the final abandonment. They were scrapped in August and September, 1946, the bodies of Nos. 151, 155 and 158 being taken to the Plymouth Argyle football ground at Home Park for use as pavilions. The three bogie cars which had not been re-trucked (Nos. 156, 163 and 164) had been scrapped in 1942, together with the following cars which had stood in the depot unused since 1938.

| | | |
|---|---|---|
| 2 and 6 ... | ... | ex-Exeter. |
| 10-15 ... | ... | ex-Torquay. |
| · 79 ... | ... | Permanent way car, ex-Devonport. |
| 142-144 | ... | " Square faces." |

The welding car, No. 42 (ex-demi-car) survived in a state bordering on dereliction until the autumn of 1946. The lower-deck of ex-Torquay No. 10 lies in a field at Yelverton.

### LIVERY.

The red and yellow livery was continued until 1922, when a new colour scheme of primrose yellow and white with heavy red lining was introduced. In about 1925, this was altered to unlined deep yellow and white with black lettering, and some two years later yet another livery was brought out, employing a " speckled " brown with white upperworks, gold lining and small gold lettering. Finally, in 1930, came the maroon and white finish with gold lining which became the standard livery in the closing years of the system. The bogie cars (151-166) were varnished teak all over until 1931, in consequence of which they became known to the staff as " Brown Bears." At this time, they carried the municipal coat of arms on the front panel of each dashboard as well as at each end of the waist panel, with the number displayed on each side dash panel. The latter feature also

*The late G. N. Southerden.*
No. 151 the first Corporation-built bogie car.

*The late G. N. Southerden.*
On right: No. 14 ex-Torquay bogie; on left: No. 1 ex-Exeter, at Theatre.

applied to the English Electric four-wheelers, which had similar three-panelled dashes, but these embellishments were later altered to the usual arrangement in conformity with the rest of the fleet. In their final years of life, all the bogie cars and some of the " square faces " had the rocker panel painted maroon instead of white. It is believed that Plymouth held the record among British tramway operators for the greatest number of colour schemes employed on its cars.

## Track.

A good deal of doubling was carried out by the corporation, particularly in Devonport, and by 1930 the whole system was double track throughout except for the West Hoe section, Union Street and the former interlaced track at Morice Town, the latter having been replaced by plain single track. These sections were not signalled as all the loops were within sight of one another. A siding was laid in at the Guildhall.

There were several methods of point control and operation in use at junctions and these, together with the corresponding overhead line installations, are indicated on the small map by the letters A to G, viz:

A. Automatic point control: overhead worked by swinging bar device.

B. Both operated by car crews.

C. Points operated from roadside, overhead by pull-off cord.

D. Points operated by crew but overhead as A.

E. Points fitted with return rubber blocks, overhead as A.

F. Points operated by switchman, overhead as C.

G. Automatic trolley reverser.

## Current Collection.

The whole of the overhead suspension was converted from bracket arm to span wire construction from 1920 onwards except on the three sections which had a common bracket for both wires. The wire used was of grooved section with mechanical ears. Junction arrangements are, for convenience, detailed with the map references in the preceding paragraph.

## Depots.

The Milehouse Depot of the ex-Devonport & District system was chosen as the administrative headquarters and chief depot of the combined system and suitably enlarged for the purpose. Two additional sheds containing three roads each were built on to the front of the original premises between 1921 and 1923, and a third, having the same number of tracks, was completed by 1927. The original sheds at the rear were turned into workshops and new offices were built, the entire layout covering an area of seven acres.

Prince Rock was retained as a subsidiary depot and the others were sold. Stonehouse became the warehouse of a tyre concern; Millbay was converted into a sweet factory and was "blitzed" in 1941; while Compton is now a transport contractor's garage, four white stones on the front still marking the original height of the roof when it was a horse-car shed. Since the abandonment of the tramways, Prince Rock Depot has been demolished and the site built over, while the corrugated-iron structure at Camel's Head is now a garage with its two tracks still inside. Milehouse is now the Corporation's bus garage, some of the trackwork still being in place.

# SWINDON

This small Wiltshire system (the only one in that county) was operated electrically by the Swindon Corporation throughout its existence. It consisted of three short routes radiating from the New Town, and the outer termini were (i) Rodbourne, at a point just short of the Gloucester line railway bridge; (ii) Gorse Hill, approximately opposite the Isolation Hospital; and (iii) the Corn Exchange, Old Town. There was also a spur along Wellington Street to the G.W.R. Junction Station, and the total length of the route was 3 miles 5 furlongs 5.7 chains.

The focal point of the system for service purposes was the junction at the corner of Fleet Street and Bridge Street, and although only a plain two-way single-line junction situated in narrow streets, this point was rather ambitiously named "The Centre"! The three-way junction at the top of Milford Street was actually less important as the curve from Wellington Street into Manchester Road was used only by cars from the station to reach the depot.

The necessary powers for its construction were granted in a Tramway Order issued in 1901 and Dick, Kerr & Co. were appointed contracters. The entire system was opened on 22nd September, 1904, the inaugural car being driven by the Mayor, Alderman Hinton.

The system remained unchanged throughout its life, and the only incident of note occurred on the evening of 1st June, 1906, when car No. 11, heavily laden, ran away down the steep gradient in Victoria Road and jumped the track on the curve near the Town Hall. As a result of its overturning, four passengers were killed and 30 injured, and a Board of Trade enquiry was held.

Tramway operation by the Corporation came to an end on 11th July, 1929, when the whole of the system was given over to motor buses.

### SERVICES AND FARES.

Junction Station - Old Town.
Rodbourne - Gorse Hill.
No service numbers were used.

There was originally a flat penny fare for all three sections, but later each section was divided into two 1d. stages, viz:

Centre - Theatre - Corn Exchange.
Centre - Graham Street - Gorse Hill.
Centre - Westcott Place - Rodbourne.

Penny transfers and returns were available, but the through fare went up to 2½d. and finally 3d., the latter value being over-stamped on 2½d. tickets.

### TICKETS.

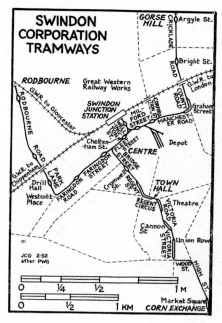

Simple geographical stages sufficed for this small system. Colours were 1d. white later yellow, 1½d. green later white, 2d. green, 2½d. and 3d. blue; transfer buff or salmon with red stripe; workmen's ½d. purple, 1d. blue, 1½d. pink; child prepaid, blue. The illustrations show a 1½d. white, 1d. transfer salmon with red stripe, and 2½d. surcharged 3d. in red, on blue.

### ROLLING STOCK.

The fleet consisted of 13 double-deck four-wheeled cars, all of which had open tops and balconies. The main batch, delivered by Dick, Kerr & Co. for the opening, was numbered 1-9 and had three side windows, 48 seats, D.K. equipment and Brill 21E trucks. These originally had reversed stairs, but direct quarter-turn stairs were later substituted. Nos. 10-12 were built by Brush in 1913 and were larger and more powerful cars having four side windows and seating for 54; they were fitted with magnetic track brakes. The last addition, No. 13, was a vestibuled car supplied by Brush in 1921 and also seated 54.

Upon the abandonment of the system, all the car bodies were disposed of for £5 apiece, and two or three are still to be seen in a privately-owned recreation ground at Rodbourne Cheney. The body of No. 13 is standing complete in a field at Chiseldon, Wilts.

## LIVERY.

Maroon and cream.

## TRACK.

The system was of 3 ft. 6 in. gauge and the rails used weighed 105 lb. per yard. The track, none of which was reserved, amounted to 4.53 miles in total length and was single throughout except on the Corn Exchange section, which had three short lengths of double line.

*The late G. N. Southerden.*
No. 8 of the first batch as rebuilt, at Gorse Hill terminus.

141

The maximum gradient was the 1 in 14 in Victoria Road whereon the accident occurred, while the sharpest curve had a radius of 37 ft. There were no signals or automatic points.

## CURRENT COLLECTION.

The overhead system with swivel trolley heads was employed, suspension being by means of side poles and bracket arms, many of which are still used for street lighting. Automatic trolley reversers were installed at the termini.

## DEPOT.

This was situated on the south side of Manchester Road, on the Gorse Hill route and approximately 400 yards from the junction at Wellington Street, and had three roads and a short siding. It now forms the paint shop, stores, fitting shop and machine shop of the Corporation's motor bus garage which occupies the same site, and traces of the tram tracks remain in the machine shop.

# TAUNTON

One of the most notable things about the Taunton system was that although it was the smallest urban electric tramway undertaking in this country, it originally had the longest title. When incorporated in 1900 it was known by the impressive if cumbrous name of Taunton & West Somerset Electric Railways & Tramways Company, Ltd., from which it would seem that far-reaching operations on a large scale were envisaged by the promoters. Rather disappointingly, however, the system resolved itself into a short electric tramway, at first barely a mile in length, running from the far end of East Reach, on the main road to Bridgwater, through the town to the Great Western Railway Station. Work on its construction began early in 1901, the contractors being R. Blackwell & Co., Ltd., and the line was completed and inspected by the Board of Trade on 16th August the same year. Public services were inaugurated five days later, on the 21st August.

The company changed its title in about 1903 to the more appropriate Taunton Electric Traction Co., Ltd., and the undertaking was a member of the British Electric Traction group.

It is evident that the construction was carried out somewhat too hurriedly, for by the spring of 1905 the track had got into a bad state and had to be relaid throughout. During the time of reconstruction the service was temporarily suspended and the company's staff were taken on by the contractors. Shortly afterwards, powers were obtained for an extension northwards from the railway station along Kingston Road to Rowbarton, and this was duly opened on 13th August, 1909, the new terminus being at Salisbury Street. No further extensions were built and the total length of the line was 1.66 miles.

Current for the tramway was supplied by the Taunton Corporation by agreement with the company, and after the 1914-18 war, owing to the increased cost of electricity production, the Corporation sought to revise the terms of the agreement. The company, however, declined to consider any increase in the charges, and the Corporation thereupon obtained an Order in court to have the agreement annulled, informing the company that unless fresh terms could be negotiated, the power supply would be discontinued as from 28th

143

May, 1921. Unfortunately the company maintained its attitude and so, the Corporation's threat having been duly carried out, the trams ceased running on the date specified and the undertaking was subsequently wound up.

Taunton's was the second electric tramway in this country to be totally abandoned, having been preceded by Sheerness-on-Sea four years earlier. Even so, during its brief lifetime, the Taunton trams carried some 15 million passengers.

## SERVICES AND FARES.

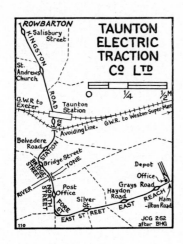

The normal working headway was 7½-10 minutes, increased to 6-7½ minutes on Saturdays and at other busy times. The through fare from East Reach to Rowbarton was 2d. and from East Reach to the Station and Silver Street to Rowbarton was 1½d., intermediate stages being a penny.

## TICKETS.

The small system needed only a small range of tickets which were full geographical. Colours were 1d. white, and 1½d. green, later brown, 2d. pink. ½d. workmen blue and ½d. child yellow were issued in books of 12 and 6 respectively.

## ROLLING STOCK.

The original fleet consisted of six double-deck four-wheelers built and supplied by Brush with their own trucks and equipment. These were of the open-top balcony design typical of the period and had four arched-top windows per side, reversed stairs and very shallow dashes with the handbrake fitted on the outside. They had seats for 50 passengers (26 outside and 24 in the saloon) and carried the headlamps on the upper deck front sheeting.

When the line was undergoing reconstruction, these cars were sold to the Leamington and Warwick Tramways and were replaced at Taunton by six single-deckers with which the service was resumed in 1905. It has sometimes been suggested that this change in rolling stock coincided with the extension to Rowbarton and was necessitated by the railway bridge at the station being too low to clear double-deck cars, but the single-deckers were, in fact, introduced before the

*G. W. Copeland.*
No. 5 in East Reach depot in 1904. Mr. Smith, General Manager, on
upper deck.

extension was made. They were again of Brush manufacture throughout and were strongly reminiscent of contemporary American practice,
having four rectangular side windows, a monitor roof and the headlamp on the canopy. Originally these cars had the bulkheads behind
the second and fourth window pillars, making a short centre saloon
with unenclosed seats at each end, the two end " windows " actually
being unglazed. Later, these were glazed and end bulkheads fitted,
although the original ones were retained. The cars were also given
advertisement boards around the roof and one of them had an over-
head-line inspection tower rigged on it.

When the system was closed down three of these cars were sold to
the Torquay Tramways Company, who converted them for one-man
operation. Of the other three, the trucks were sent to the B.E.T.
system at Gravesend & Northfleet and the bodies disposed of locally
for use as bungalows, etc.

### LIVERY.

Dark lake and cream, with the familiar B.E.T. magnet and wheel
device displayed on the side panels. Lining and other exterior decoration was simplified in later years.

145

## TRACK.

The line was built to the 3 ft. 6 in. gauge and the rails used weighed 90 lb. per yard. The track was single throughout with ten passing loops, and amounted to exactly two miles. The line was laid entirely in streets but the only sharp curve was the entrance to the depot, which had a radius of 35 feet. Gradients were very easy, the maximum being 1 in 25.

## CURRENT COLLECTION.

The orthodox overhead trolley system was used, but an unusual feature was that the cars always ran with the trolley rope hanging loose instead of being tied up. Overhead suspension was by means of side poles with bracket arms except along East Reach and North

146

*Brush, courtesy E. W. Griffiths.*
Single-deck car No. 6 as delivered by Brush.

Street, where span wires were used. The original installation employed 1 gauge round section wire with soldered ears, but in 1919 this was replaced by 2 gauge grooved wire with mechanical ears. Power was drawn from the Corporation generating station in St. James' Street and fed to the line there and at Silver Street. Two breaker boxes may still be seen, one being in North Street near the bridge over the Tone, and the other opposite the County Hospital in East Reach. All the poles are also still in place, showing the B.E.T. device.

### DEPOT.

This was located at the East Reach terminus and lay approximately 100 yards to the north of the road between Alfred Street and Leycroft Road. It measured approximately 120 feet by 35 feet and had three roads, one of which had an inspection pit with jacking equipment. Repair and paint shops were provided at the rear and were complete with lathe, grinder, wheel press and a small forge. The premises are now used as a store by the local distributors of a well-known brand of fruit drink.

# TORQUAY

There were no tramways in this popular seaside resort until the early years of the present century, when the Torquay Tramways Company, Ltd. was formed for the purpose of constructing and operating a system of electric tramways in the borough. The company was a subsidiary of the National Electrical Construction Co., Ltd., of Laurence Pountney Hill, London, who were also responsible for promoting the Mexborough & Swinton and Dewsbury & Ossett systems in Yorkshire and the Rhondda Valley Tramways in South Wales.

The necessary powers were granted in a Tramways Order dated August, 1904, and the work of track laying commenced at Torre Station on 23rd October, 1905, the contractors being the British Thompson-Houston Co., Ltd. Three of the authorised routes, namely those from Beacon Quay to Torre Station via Union Street, Brunswick Square to St. Marychurch via Upton, and St. Marychurch to

*Torquay Times and Devonshire Press Ltd.*
Beacon Quay on opening day. Dolter system.

Union Street via Ellacombe, were opened for traffic in April, 1907. The remaining line—Strand to St. Marychurch via Wellswood and Babbacombe—suffered some delay as the road at Torwood Mount had to be widened in order to take the tramway, and this service was not inaugurated until November, 1907.

A scheme was then put forward for the construction of a line along Torbay Road to the Grand Hotel, the latter point also serving Torquay Station. This was duly approved and powers were granted on 7th January, 1908. Construction work was started on 11th February the same year and the line opened on 16th April following. An extension of this route to the borough boundary just south of Livermead was approved by the Torquay Town Council on 3rd November, 1909, but it was subsequently decided to negotiate with the neighbouring Paignton Urban District Council with a view to the tramway being carried further along the coast road to Paignton Station. The scheme was finally agreed to by the authorities concerned and a through service of trams from Torquay Station to Paignton Station was put in operation on 17th July, 1911, immediately after the new line had been declared fit for public use by the Board of Trade inspector, Major Pringle.

No further extensions were made by the company and the final route length of the whole system was 9.24 miles.

The undertaking was carried on successfully for over 20 years, but after the war, the company began to feel the pinch of bus competition, chiefly on the part of the Devon General Omnibus & Touring Co., Ltd.

In 1922 the Tramways Company acquired a controlling interest in the " Devon General " and transferred to them the few buses which it was operating. Despite this co-ordination, the rapid build-up of the bus services in the area proved fatal to the trams and ultimately it was decided, with the sanction of the two local authorities concerned, to abandon the system in favour of " Devon General " buses. To these, the trams succumbed during January, 1934, the Paignton route being closed on the 14th and the rest of the system on the 31st of that month.

### SERVICE AND FARES.

The basic services operated were as follows:
Strand-Paignton.
Strand-Ellacombe-St. Marychurch-Wellswood-Strand, circular.
Reverse of previous route.
Beacon Quay-Union Street-Torre Station.
Torre Station-Upton-St. Marychurch.
During the busy summer season, the company used its circular

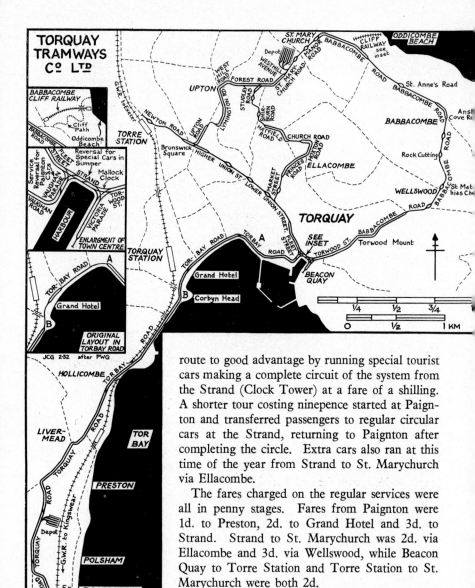

route to good advantage by running special tourist cars making a complete circuit of the system from the Strand (Clock Tower) at a fare of a shilling. A shorter tour costing ninepence started at Paignton and transferred passengers to regular circular cars at the Strand, returning to Paignton after completing the circle. Extra cars also ran at this time of the year from Strand to St. Marychurch via Ellacombe.

The fares charged on the regular services were all in penny stages. Fares from Paignton were 1d. to Preston, 2d. to Grand Hotel and 3d. to Strand. Strand to St. Marychurch was 2d. via Ellacombe and 3d. via Wellswood, while Beacon Quay to Torre Station and Torre Station to St. Marychurch were both 2d.

### TICKETS.

The colour scheme was fairly consistent being 1½d. white, 2d. blue, 2½d. pink, 3d. yellow, 4d. purple. Workmen's singles were in the same colour as the ordinary tickets covering that stage—½d. white, 1d. blue, 1½d. yellow. Child tickets had coloured

edges; exchange tickets were old gold or violet. Illustrated are 2d. 5116, an early full geographical with pale mauve overprint on the lower half: note the centrally printed stages with the conditions of issue in the marginal gutters—the reverse of the usual practice. 3d. straw 8596, a later issue with the stages arranged in two columns. 1d. child 1967, white with green edges and red overprint. 9d. circular 7649, white with blue stripe, covered a comprehensive tour of Torquay, including a trip on the Babbacombe Cliff Railway. Day of issue shown by bell punch on right, and various sections as used cancelled by hand clippers on left. 6242 is an exchange in old gold with red overprint. 3d. 0588 is deep purple with black R and was issued on the Cliff Railway during tramway ownership. 6d. 34047 shows an "Automaticket" issued by the Corporation covering a return fare for *two* persons. 2d. 10963 brown was issued by the *Borough* of Torquay for one up single.

## ROLLING STOCK.

The initial fleet was supplied by Brush in 1907 and consisted of 18 open-top four-wheel cars, mounted on Mountain & Gibson radial trucks with 8 ft. 6 in. wheelbase. The bodies had three side windows and seated 49 passengers (27/22), the seats in the balconies originally being transverse instead of curved in the usual way as they were later. The equipment was supplied by B.T.H. and comprised their B.18 controllers and two 35 h.p. motors per car.

In 1929 cars, 1, 7 and 16 were re-trucked on short-wheelbase Brill 21E rigids, while 9 and 10 were given the same type of truck but with a long wheelbase in 1931 and 1930 respectively; Nos. 17 and 18 also appear to have been fitted with the latter type of truck, but exactly when is not known.

Cars 19-33 followed in 1910 for the Paignton line and were of the same type and specification as the previous series and by the same makers; they differed, however, in having Brill 21E trucks (short wheelbase) from the first and appear always to have had transverse canopy seats. Both batches carried ornate iron grillework around the upper deck.

In 1921, three four-wheeled single-deckers were purchased second-hand from the Taunton Electric Traction Co., Ltd. and adapted for one-man operation by alteration to the dash and steps. These became Nos. 34-36 in the Torquay fleet and were used mainly on the Torre Station-St. Marychurch route.

The next and final additions came in 1923-5 when Brush supplied six open-top bogie cars on maximum-traction trucks. These were vestibuled units of a much improved design and were numbered

*M. J. O'Connor.*
Bogie car of 37-40 class near the Pavilion.

*The late G. N. Southerden.*
St. Marychurch depot with single-deck car No. 34 (ex-Taunton demi-car) on extreme right.

No. 8 with original pivotal truck.

No. 14 at Torre Station.  Dolter system.

*Courtesy R. C. Sambourne.*
Trams operating on the stud system.

37-42. The first four had five side windows and 76 seats and were fitted with Hoffman roller bearings, the latter making them among the smoothest running cars in the West County. Nos. 41 and 42 seated four less but had transverse seats in the saloon and controllers with " dead man's handle " equipment; they also differed in having the indicators set lower over the guard rails, and wire netting instead of ironwork around the upper deck.

An unusual feature of the Torquay cars was an oil lamp fitted at the nearside top of the saloon bulkhead on the platform side. These were provided for emergency use in the event of a power failure. Mechanical slipper brakes were standard throughout the fleet on account of the steep gradients. All the double-deck cars had red plush seating on the lower deck except Nos. 41 and 42, which had a blue and grey fabric.

Cars 37-42 and six of the four-wheelers (Nos. 7, 9, 10, 16, 17 and 18) were sold to Plymouth Corporation in 1933 and the rest of the stock was scrapped.

### LIVERY.

The cars were painted maroon on the waist panel, sole bar, dash and stairs, lined in gold or yellow, and cream on the rocker, pillars and upper deck sheeting. By 1929 the cream had given place to canary yellow (on some cars the new colour was almost orange)

155

and the elaborate corner embellishments in the lining were dropped. Numerals were carried out in gold relieved with pink (some with blue) and the large lettering on the rocker panels was in gold, shaded blue.

## CURRENT COLLECTION.

The local system in Torquay was originally equipped on the Dolter surface-contact system, in which energised metal studs placed in the road between the running rails made contact with a magnetised skate beneath the car. This was adopted on account of public objection to overhead wires but did not work well—either in Torquay or in the few other towns which tried it—and the 1909 Order for the construction of the Paignton line stipulated that the Dolter or any other surface contact system was not to be employed; the overhead trolley system having been decided upon for this extension, the Order also authorised the conversion of the Strand-Grand Hotel section to this form of traction so as to enable a through service to be operated without interruption.

An enquiry into the operation of the Dolter system on the earlier lines was opened on 23rd May, 1910, and in the following September it was decided to convert the whole of the tramways to overhead trolley working. Following upon an inspection by Major Pringle in March, 1911, the Board of Trade issued a certificate to the company assenting to this conversion subject to the latter's compliance with certain conditions. The change-over was completed later the same year, the cars originally fitted with Dolter equipment (Nos. 1-18) being adapted for trolley operation.

## TRACK.

The system was of 3 ft. 6 in. gauge and comprised about 16 miles of track. The bulk of the local system in Torquay itself was of single-and-loop construction but the section in Torbay Road between the points marked A and B on the map was doubled in 1926 and the Paignton extension was double throughout. The track was laid entirely in streets and the rails used weighed 90 lb. per yard. The steepest gradient was a section of 1 in 10 in Ellacombe and the sharpest curve had a radius of 31 feet. All points were single-tongued and junctions were operated by the motormen except at Market Street, where a pointsman was employed. Electric light signals were originally installed on the single-and-loop section between Forest Road and Hatfield Road, Ellacombe, but these were later disused and automatic semaphores were provided to protect the single line in Hatfield Road only. On the St. Marychurch-Wellswood section, the single line immediately north of St. Matthias Church was also signalled.

The overhead construction embodied side poles with bracket arms over most of the local system and span wires on the Paignton route with centre poles along the Strand. The poles are still used for street lighting except in Upton Road, Shirburn Road and the main central streets in Torquay itself.

## DEPOTS.

The chief depot was located in Westhill Avenue, St. Marychurch, and had six roads including workshops. It is now used by the Torquay Corporation for its refuse lorries, etc. A smaller car shed having four roads was built at Preston, on the outskirts of Paignton and this is now a garage, having had a shop with offices over, erected on what was once the depot yard.

# BABBACOMBE CLIFF RAILWAY

In addition to the street tramways, the company operated a cable railway running down the cliffs from Babbacombe Downs to Oddicombe Beach. This was constructed by Waygood Otis, Ltd., the well-known lift makers, at a cost of £15,648 and opened on 1st April, 1926.

The line was built by the Torquay Corporation and leased to the Tramway Company for operation, and following upon the latter's demise, the working of the line was taken over by the Corporation in April, 1935.

The line is 720 feet long and has a gradient of 1 in 2.84. It operates on the counterbalance principle with one pair of cars, to each of which is attached a cable consisting of four 2½ in. diameter steel wire ropes. This cable leads through reduction pulley gearing powered by a 45 b.h.p. D.C. variable speed motor, which develops 325-650 r.p.m. A mercury arc rectifier is installed so that power can, if necessary, be drawn from the A.C. mains. A steel safety cable is also attached to each car so that in the event of the main one failing, the tension on the safety cable would cause a spring-loaded mechanism to operate, forcing steel teeth on the car underframe to lock on the track. The line is worked from the upper station by manual control of the switchgear operating the motor, and the cars are stopped automatically from the track.

The track foundation is formed of four longitudinal concrete beams, 17 in. deep and 10 in. wide, carrying 10 in. by 5 in. timbers, on which transverse sleepers are laid. The rails are of flat-bottom section weighing 105 lb. per yard and are spiked down. A station and waiting room is provided at each terminus but there are no intermediate stations. Near the lower terminus, the line crosses the cliff road on an overbridge.

The car bodies are of tramcar pattern with end doors and seat 20 passengers each. They are finished externally in maroon and cream and are carried on a four-wheeled triangular underframe with inside bearings.

During the busy summer season for which it operated, the railway proved popular and remunerative and prior to the late war, carried an average of 192,000 passengers per annum. The fares charged were 2d. single and 3d. return and the average yearly revenue was about £2,000. The statement of accounts for the line for the years 1937 to 1941 shows that only one year resulted in a deficit, that being 1940, when revenue dropped to £986. It returned to normal in the following year, but owing to war conditions, the service was then suspended entirely. The line unfortunately suffered much from its enforced disuse, and adverse conditions and high costs since the war prevented its reconstruction until recently. It was reopened on 29th June, 1951, and the only change is that the cars are now painted cream and green.

Cars on the Babbacombe cliff railway.        *Chapman, Dawlish.*

# WESTON-SUPER-MARE

The Weston-Super-Mare & District Electric Supply Co., Ltd., a member of the B.E.T. group obtained a Tramways Order in 1900 authorising it to construct and operate 3.71 miles of electric tramways in the town, which, up to then, had had no tram service of any kind. Two of the authorised sections, namely Milton Road and Station Road, were not proceeded with, but the remainder was constructed by R. Blackwell & Co., Ltd., and comprised three routes. These radiated from the corner of Oxford Street and Beach Road to Locking Road, Old Pier and West of England Sanatorium respectively, amounting in all to 2.92 route miles. The two latter sections spanned the length of the promenade, while the Locking Road line ran inland to the back of the town.

Single-deck toast-rack car. Note length of trolley boom.

The official opening ceremony took place at 12 noon on Monday, 12th May, 1902 (four days earlier than planned), when the first car was driven from Ashcombe Road to the Pier Hotel carrying members and officials of the local Council and representatives of the Press. A ten-minute service was maintained over that section for the rest of the day and it is recorded that 3,973 passengers were carried. Regular services commenced over the whole of the system on the following Saturday, 17th May.

The undertaking remained unchanged in operation and administration until 1935, when the system was sold to the Bristol Tramways & Carriage Co., Ltd. An agreement was subsequently made with the local Council whereby the trams were replaced by motor buses operated by the Bristol Company and the system was closed entirely on Saturday, 17th April, 1937. At 10.15 p.m. on that day, the last car (No. 8) was driven from the Grand Pier to the Depot by Mr. J. G. Western, Chairman of the Weston-Super-Mare U.D.C., its progress being followed by dozens of motor cars and cyclists and cheered by a large gathering of people. There were, of course, the pranks and souvenir-scrounging usually met with on such occasions! The car was not decorated, but Mr. George Simons, Vice-Chairman of the Council, armed with punch and cash bag, distributed special

*Sandys, Ltd.*

Two-rack and double-decker car at Old Pier.

tickets to the passengers, and the proceeds of the final run were sent to the Weston-Super-Mare Hospital.

The Weston system was very successful for a small undertaking and carried heavy traffic in the summer season, when the promenade route was a great attraction to visitors. During their lifetime, the cars ran 4 million miles and carried 51 million passengers.

The company itself continued to function purely as an electric supply concern until the recent nationalisation of the industry.

### SERVICES AND FARES.

The Sanatorium and Old Pier routes were operated together as a through service, and additional workings (usually with the "toastrack" cars) were run between the Old Pier and Grand Pier only during the busy summer months. The Locking Road section was operated at all times as a shuttle service to and from Oxford Street, more often than not by car No. 1, and "extras" were put on for the Excursion Station when the occasion demanded. Originally, there was no Sunday service until 2 p.m.

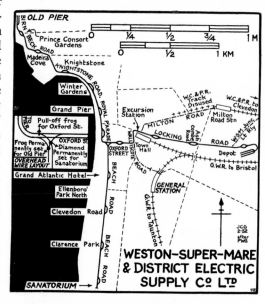

The original fares were 1d. for Locking Road and 2d. for any distance on the sea front service, but on account of bus competition commencing in about 1926, penny fares were made available on these cars also. The penny stages were Old Pier-Grand Pier, Madeira Cove-Ellenborough Park North and Grand Pier-Sanatorium.

### TICKETS.

No definite colour schemes can be traced. Those illustrated are 2d. white 9998 an early issue. 1d. white 4444 a very austere late '20s' issue. 1d. pale blue with green overprint at the bottom 1242 the final type is fully geographical. The 1½d. and 2d. in this series were purple and white respectively. Note in all cases the hand

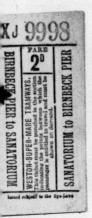 

clipper cancellation. Also illustrated is a 1½d. on pink paper issued in booklets.

### ROLLING STOCK.

The fleet put into service in 1902 consisted of 16 four-wheeled cars built by Brush and having Brill 21E 6 ft. wheelbase trucks and B.T.H. equipment incorporating two 25 h.p. motors per car. Twelve of these (Nos. 1-12) were open-top double-deckers with four side windows, reversed stairs, and a seating capacity of 50 (28/22), while Nos. 13-16 were roofed single-deck " toastracks " seating 44 passengers on ten crossbenches between the bulkheads and one on each platform. These cars all had the handbrake mounted outside the dash.

On the night of Thursday, 10th September, 1903, a fierce gale sprang up and threw great seas over the promenade, which was then immediately alongside the Beach Road tramway and not separated from it by a grass strip as now. The yacht *Sweetheart* was also carried on to the roadway by the seas and its mast became entangled with the overhead wires, causing a short-circuit and bringing the trams to a standstill. Four open-top cars on the promenade were damaged, their motors and lower decks being flooded, and several passengers received electric shocks. The cars were towed to the depot that night, but as the necessary repair facilities were not available there, they were sold to the larger B.E.T. system at Swansea.

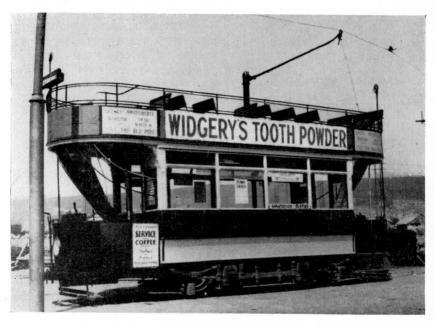

*Weston-Super-Mare Electric Supply Co., Ltd.*
Double-deck car in depot yard.

The remaining eight cars of this type were re-grouped 1-8 and the numbers 9-12 were never used again.

To the remaining 12 cars were added, in 1927, two more " toast-racks," similar to the earlier ones but larger and having a plain curved roof without the raised centre. These were again Brush built and seated 52 on 11 crossbenches between the bulkheads and one on each platform. Their trucks were Brill patent " Radiax " models with a 9 ft. wheelbase and B.T.H. supplied the equipment. They received the numbers 17 and 18.

No further cars were purchased after these and the stock remained at a total of 14 cars until abandonment. None of them was ever vesti-buled or structurally altered in any way. The single-deckers were kept almost exclusively on the Old Pier-Sanatorium route. The lower decks of three of the open-toppers (latterly reduced to mere skeletons) stood until recently in the fields adjacent to the main Weston-Bristol road near Worle, and that of No. 7, shorn of both canopies, still does duty as a store in the depot.*

*It was broken up in 1951.

## LIVERY.

The cars were finished in the standard crimson lake and cream of the B.E.T. group, with the addition of grey on the upper-deck panelling of Nos. 1-8.

## TRACK.

This was of 4 ft. 8½ in. gauge and totalled 3.53 miles. Rails of 90 lb. per yard section were used and the track was single throughout with 14 passing loops, the whole of it being laid in streets. Until Beach Road was widened in about 1926, the tramway was laid on the seaward edge of the road close to a stone wall. The only gradient was a short stretch of 1 in 25 in Birnbeck Road, and the radius of the sharpest curve was 42 feet. During the winter, Old Pier cars reversed at the last loop before the terminus.

## CURRENT COLLECTION.

By overhead trolley with swivel heads, employing side pole and bracket suspension throughout. The overhead equipment at the Oxford Street junction is shown on the accompanying map, the frog permanently set for the curve towards the pier being of interest. So much " fiddling " was required to get a trolley round the sealed-off curve that cars from the Sanatorium returning to the depot normally used the other one and reversed on the pier side. The single-deckers were remarkable for the length of their trolleys, these being mounted direct on the car roof instead of being upheld on a standard. All cars carried a trolley rope, but on the single-deckers this was kept wound around the arm and a bamboo pole used instead. Most of the poles and brackets are still in use for street lighting.

## DEPOT.

This was situated at the Locking Road terminus adjoining the Electricity Works, of which it now forms part. It had four roads, each of which could take four cars: the toastrack cars were generally stored on the northernmost pair of lines.

In passing, it is of interest to note that the system was in close proximity to the Weston, Clevedon & Portishead Light Railway, which was itself originally incorporated under the Tramways Act, 1870. As far as is known, this line was always intended to be a steam-operated light railway but in 1897 it did make an attempt at justifying its tramway leanings by laying a track along the side of the then undeveloped Milton Road towards the centre of Weston, doubtless with a view to reaching the sea front. This was never used, however, and the track was soon taken up. If the Weston Company had built its Milton Road section, or if a separate enterprise authorised in the Weston-Super-Mare Junction Light Railway Order of 1910 for a connection between the Locking Road tramway and the W.C. & P. line near its terminus (a gap of only 400 yards or so) had come to fruition, we might have seen some interesting through running, which certainly would have been beneficial to both systems, particularly as the Locking Road section was always the " Cinderella " of the Weston tramways. As it was, however, the two remained " so near and yet so far " and the light railway was itself closed to all traffic in May, 1940.

*Sandys, Ltd.*
Toastrack car No 17 on Brill Radiax truck. Parts of this car still survived in the boiler house at Locking Road in 1953.

# WORCESTER

The first tramways in this city were horse-operated by the Worcester Tramways Company, Limited, who, under powers granted in orders under the Tramways Act issued in 1881, 1885, 1887 and 1890, constructed lines from the Cross to the Vine Hotel, Barbourne; to "The Portobello" in Bransford Road, St. John's; and to Shrub Hill Station. These amounted to some four route miles and were opened in 1882. A new concern, named Worcester Tramways, Ltd., purchased the undertaking in 1894 and was later itself acquired by the Worcester Electric Traction Co., Ltd., a subsidiary of the British Electric Traction Co., Ltd., and registered on 22nd August, 1902. The B.E.T. had opened negotiations with the Worcester Corporation in 1901 for a concession to operate the tramways electrically, with the result that the Worcester Tramways Act and the Worcester &

*Courtesy H. V. Jinks.*

Horse tram.

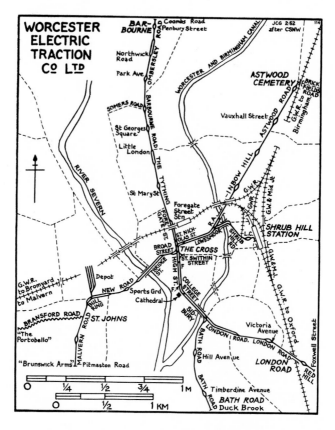

District Light Railways Order, both of 1901, gave the company powers to operate electric tramways within the city for a period of 28 years as from 1st May, 1901, at the expiration of which the Corporation was granted an option to purchase the undertaking. The Worcester (Extension) Light Railways Order, 1902, authorised the construction of additional lines. The tramways accordingly passed into the hands of the Worcester Electric Traction Co., Ltd. on 31st October, 1902, and the horse-cars ceased running the following year.

Construction work on the electric system was pressed forward rapidly and the official opening took place on 6th February, 1904, with services to Barbourne, Shrub Hill and St. John's. The last-named route took on an altered form with its electrification, as the original track along Bransford Road was abandoned and the new line was instead carried on down the Malvern Road to the " Brunswick Arms."

Three new routes were constructed at the same time, of which

*Courtesy H. V. Jinks.*
Original type of car on St. John's route.

the first to be opened was that to the Cemetery via Rainbow Hill.
The others ran southwards from The Cross to London Road and
Bath Road and were opened in April, 1904, and on 20th June, 1904,
respectively. An extension of the St. John's route along Malvern
Road was brought into use on 25th August, 1906, and a terminal
spur in St. Swithin Street to relieve congestion at The Cross completed
the system. The total route and track mileages were then 5.86 and
8.58 respectively.

In 1926, the Worcester Corporation obtained an Act of Parliament
authorising it to purchase the tramways as a going concern, and either
to operate the system itself (powers also being granted for trackless
trolley vehicles and motor buses) or alternatively to lease their powers.
The Corporation sought the advice of the late Mr. A. Baker, then
General Manager of the Birmingham Corporation Tramways &
Omnibus Department, who recommended that tram operation be

continued for the time being and that later a change-over to trackless trolley vehicles be made, with motor buses to develop new routes. This advice was not accepted, however, and instead the Corporation decided to lease the undertaking to the Birmingham & Midland Motor Omnibus Co., Ltd. for 21 years. Negotiations then commenced with the Worcester Electric Traction Company for the purchase of the tramways, the purchase price being agreed at £58,000 plus the stores at valuation.

The entire tramway system ceased operation on 31st May, 1928, and the B.M.M.O. bus services commenced on the following day. In recording the passing of the Worcester trams it is of interest to note that in their heyday, they carried a yearly average of 3,000,000 passengers—an impressive figure for so small a system.

### SERVICES.

The Barbourne and St. John's routes were operated together as a cross-city service, while London Road and Bath Road cars reversed in St. Swithin Street, and Cemetery and Shrub Hill cars in St. Nicholas Street.

There was originally a uniform fare of one penny from the city centre to any suburban terminus, but in 1920 this was increased to 1½d. except on the Shrub Hill and London Road routes, on which the old fare was unaltered. Malvern Road also had a penny fare to St. John's.

### TICKETS.

A simple set of tickets sufficed. 1d. and later 1½d. from each terminus to the Cross were white or blue according to the group of routes. The exchange was white with a central blue stripe.

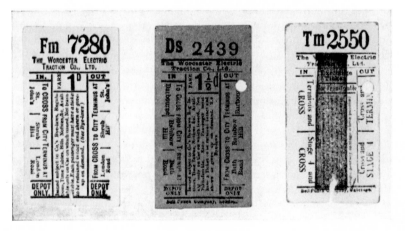

*Courtesy H. V. Jinks.*
No. 17 as supplied in 1921.

### ROLLING STOCK.

Owing to delay in delivery from the builders, the requisite number of cars was not available for the opening of the electrified system and this was accordingly carried out with the assistance of several cars borrowed from the nearby and associated Birmingham & Midland Tramways Joint Committee.

The company's own fleet as finally put into service comprised 15 open-top balcony cars of the conventional type for that period. These were built by Brush and had four windows per side and seating for 22 in the saloon and 28 outside. The stairs were of the direct half-turn design and roller indicators were fitted above the front guard rails on the upper deck. The equipment was supplied by Dick, Kerr and included two 25 h.p. motors per car, whilst the trucks were of the

171

Brush 6 ft. wheelbase ¾ spring pattern. The cars were fitted with driver's screens in 1919, these having a somewhat "makeshift" appearance and covering only the front of the platform.

In 1921, the fleet was strengthened by the addition of two further open-top four-wheeled cars. These, numbered 16 and 17, were of the same design and seating capacity as the earlier ones and were fitted from the first with a similar though rather more substantial type of semi-vestibule. The bodies of these cars were constructed in the Birmingham & Midland Joint Committee's car works at Tividale and upon delivery at the Worcester Company's depot, were mounted on Brush trucks (these having been lengthened since delivery to 7 ft. wheelbase) and fitted with English Electric equipment. They had a roller blind indicator fitted to the nearside of the saloon bulkhead facing the platform—a position of doubtful usefulness but much favoured by the Joint Committee. After the abandonment of the system, these two cars were sold to the Cheltenham & District Light Railway, but what became of them when the latter ceased to operate trams in the following year is not known for certain.

### LIVERY.

The cars were finished in holly green for the dash, waist panel and

*Courtesy H. V. Jinks.*

No. 4 on test near St. John's.

stairs, and cream for the rocker panel and all parts above the waist. The number appeared twice on each dash, either side of the head-lamp.

## TRACK.

The horse tramways are believed to have been laid to the 3 ft. gauge, but the electric system was built on the 3 ft. 6 in. gauge, using rails weighing 94 lb. per yard. Approximately three-fifths of the track was single and the gradients on the eastern side of the system included one of 1 in 13. The sharpest curve was the one from the Cross into Broad Street, which had a radius of 45 ft. The tramway in Shrub Hill Road was crossed on the level by an industrial branch railway and semaphore signals were installed on the pavement to warn road traffic of the approach of a train.

## CURRENT COLLECTION.

The overhead trolley system was used, suspension being mainly by means of side poles and bracket arms, with span wires in the city centre and down to St. John's. An automatic trolley reverser was installed at the Malvern Road terminus in 1906. A number of poles are still in use for street lighting.

## DEPOT.

This was located at the Bull Ring, St. John's, during the whole existence of the tramways, the original horse car sheds being rebuilt and enlarged to four roads at the time of electrification. The company carried out all their own repairs except, latterly, the rewinding of armatures.